SPIRITUAL GIFTS
Your Job Description From God

A GUIDE FOR THE DEVELOPMENT OF LAY MINISTRIES

Dr. Owen Weston's Class Notes

Printed in the United States of America, MCMXCVI, MMII

ISBN # 0-911866-30-2

Table of Contents

Preface

This manual has been compiled from Dr. Weston's class notes and student research over the past several years. It is a tool which incorporates a large amount of material into a systematic presentation to facilitate learning.

All Scripture references are from the New International Version (NIV) unless otherwise noted.

Reference notes give credit to the authors of the works cited and are recommended reading for the serious student who wants to learn more about the subject matter. This manual is being used around the world by churches, colleges, pastors, and teachers, and has been called the most thorough comparative study on the spiritual gifts available to date. Permission to use this material must be obtained from Dr. Owen C. Weston and LifeSprings Resources.

Introduction

The Why of Biblical New Testament Gifts

One of the first things Jesus Christ did when beginning His ministry was to read His job description from God to those in the synagogue of His hometown, Nazareth.

> The Spirit of the Lord is on me,
> because he has anointed me
> to preach good news to the poor.
> He has sent me to proclaim freedom for
> the prisoners
> and recovery of sight for the blind,
> to release the oppressed,
> to proclaim the year of the Lord's favor.
>
> Luke 4:18,19

The best clue Christians have as to what God expects of us individually (our job description) is knowing our spiritual gifts. Contrary to the practice of most churches, Paul says we must not be ignorant about spiritual gifts (1 Corinthians 12:1). He goes on to say that it is the Holy Spirit who decides who gets what gift (1 Corinthians 12:11) and that our gifts are given to us to help the Church.

If a church is to grow and reproduce itself in the normal New Testament pattern, it must be open and sensitive to the moving of the Holy Spirit. It must be accepting of the gifts from the Holy Spirit.

> He remains the Spirit of wind and fire; he remains sovereign in the Church, and is not to be boxed up in any ecclesiastical compartment. . . . And it is perfectly evident from the widespread growth of the Pentecostal Church and the neo-Pentecostal movement in the last fifty years that God has poured out these gifts in rich measure on his people, rationalistic and skeptical though we have been about them.[1]

The Bible says that every Christian has received a gift (see I Peter 4:10 and Romans 12:6) and that "to each one the manifestation of the Spirit is given for the common good" (1 Corinthians. 12:7).

It is important for each Christian to discover, develop, and use his/her gift(s) to help fulfill the mission of building the Church. A spiritual gift is the ability that the Holy

Spirit gives to Spirit-filled Christians so that they can witness even with signs and wonders (Acts 1:8) and proclaim the words and insight (1 Peter 4:10-12) supernaturally obtainable from God.

The How of Biblical New Testament Gifts

Spiritual gifts are not so divine that there is no human effort, and not so human that there is no divine intervention. It is this tension between the "Human" and the "Divine" within the individual that we call the "Inclinational Dilemma." It is also for this reason Paul says ". . . weigh carefully what is said . . ." (1 Cor. 14:29). He says this because the *human* often gets in the way of the divine. This is also the reason many people cannot operate in the supernatural or the divine. They simply will not take a step of *faith* in the *human* or *flesh*. Remember, Peter would never have stepped out of the boat onto the water without taking a *human* or *fleshly* step of faith. He had to hear and obey in the flesh before he saw the supernatural. Moses had to do the same in raising his *human* arm, holding the shepherd's rod, before God did a miracle. It seems God calls and then we must respond in faith, through the *human* or *fleshly*, before God does the divine or supernatural. Far more people would see the supernatural happen if they were willing to obey the Lord and take the *fleshly* step of faith. However, because it is a *fleshly* or *human* step, as Paul says, it must be " . . . weighed carefully . . ." Many people have not been born again, been filled with the Holy Spirit, or experienced the supernatural because they have not obeyed God's voice and taken a *human* or *fleshly* step of faith. This is particularly true in operating in the Spiritual gifts.

Understanding This Workbook

This workbook is a compilation of material from many sources. It is more a comparative study than an exegetical one. Materials used are from those used in the author's class, "Development of Lay Ministries," at Regent University.

It must be remembered that while the Bible may not include all the spiritual gifts available to us, this book is written to try to help us use the gifts that the Bible has already listed.

This book will first deal with all of the *Scriptures* that discuss the New Testament gifts. Then, it will show how authors of all faiths have *classified* these Scriptures and gifts. From these classifications, a *suggested classification* will be used to study each area and each gift. *Suggested definitions* will be given for each gift after studying what each author and the Scriptures have said about each gift. Both the *strengths* and *weaknesses* of each gift will be compared. An *Inventory test* is given to help the individual determine what gifts he or she may have. *Lists* of how the gifts could be used in the church are presented and how to get *volunteers* to use their gift. Finally, a *ten week study* synopsis of the gifts is provided to help teach the main characteristics of each gift. The following contains the *Teaching Techniques* of how to teach Spiritual Gifts.

Teaching Techniques

This material is presented so that it can be easily taught to the body of Christ. There are several methods of teaching that will help attain this goal. While the lecture method of teaching is the most common, it is not necessarily always the best method. However, if this is the method you choose, beware of its disadvantage. It tends to lead down a "one-way" street of communication. So, to enhance your lecture presentation, we encourage the use of some or all of these other techniques as well.

Brainstorming calls for spontaneous contributions by members of your group in response to a certain issue. Responses are to be "fired-off" quickly and should be recorded either on paper or on the chalkboard.

Buzz Sessions require dividing into smaller groups to discuss an issue. Appoint a chairman and a spokesman for each group. After 5 to 7 minutes, each spokesman will present the ideas of his group to the class.

Panel Discussions allow the class to get varied perspectives on an issue. Select three or four persons and tell them ahead of time what the issue will be. They should come across as well informed and certain of their opinions.

Role-Playing allows students to participate in a dramatization. Evaluate the drama and make the appropriate applications.

Press Release puts information into a style easily understood and "more digestible" in today's information-oriented society. The leader can present information in this format or can assign issues to several members of the class to come prepared to make their "press releases" to the class.

Study Format

Whether you decide to present this course during the Sunday school or Family Night hour over a quarter, or as a one-week or a one-day seminar, prepare thoroughly. Spend a lot of time getting *ready* and *set* (in prayer, and in these materials as well as other supporting documents), and then *go* for it, asking "the Spirit of Truth" to "guide you into all truth" (John 16:13).

Three Key Lists

The majority of the spiritual gifts mentioned in the Bible are found in three key chapters: 1 Corinthians 12, Romans 12, and Ephesians 4.

We will examine these three passages and list all the Gifts mentioned first before going into "secondary" passages.

1 Corinthians 12:1-26

(word of wisdom, word of knowledge, gift of faith, gifts of healing, gift of miracles, gift of prophecy, gift of discernment of spirits, gift of tongues, gift of interpretation)

Spiritual Gifts

Now about spiritual gifts, brothers, I do not want you to be ignorant. You know that when you were pagans, somehow or other you were influenced and led astray to mute idols. Therefore I tell you that no one who is speaking by the Spirit of God says, "Jesus be cursed," and no one can say, "Jesus is Lord," except by the Holy Spirit.

There are different kinds of gifts, but the same Spirit. There are different kinds of service, but the same Lord. There are different kinds of working, but the same God works all of them in all men.

Now to each one the manifestation of the Spirit is given for the common good. To one there is given through the Spirit the message of wisdom, to another the message of knowledge by means of the same Spirit, to another faith by the same Spirit, to another gifts of healing by that one Spirit, to another miraculous powers, to another prophecy, to another distinguishing between spirits, to another speaking in different kinds of tongues, and to still another the interpretation of tongues. All these are the work of one and the same Spirit, and he gives them to each one, just as he determines.

One Body, Many Parts

The body is a unit, though it is made up of many parts; and though all its parts are many, they form one body. So it is with Christ. For we were all baptized by one Spirit into one body - whether Jews or Greeks, slave or free - and we were all given the one Spirit to drink.

Now the body is not made up of one part but of many. If the foot should say, "Because I am not a hand, I do not belong to the body," it would not for that reason cease to be part of the body. And if the ear should say, "Because I am not an eye, I do not belong to the body," it would not for that reason cease to be part of the body. If the whole body were an eye, where would the sense of hearing be? If the whole body were an ear, where would the sense of smell be? But in fact God has arranged the parts in the body, every one of them, just as he wanted them to be. If they were all one part, where would the body be? As it is, there are many parts, but one body.

The eye cannot say to the hand, "I don't need you!" And the head cannot say to the feet, "I don't need you!" On the contrary, those parts of the body that seem to be weaker are indispensable, and the parts that we think are less honorable we treat with special honor. And the parts that are unpresentable are treated with special modesty, while our presentable parts need no special treatment. But God has combined the members of the body and has given greater honor to the parts that lacked it, so that there should be no division in the body, but that its parts should have equal concern for each other. If one part suffers, every part suffers with it; if one part is honored, every part rejoices with it.

1 Corinthians 12:27-31

(apostolic gift, prophetic gift, teaching gift, gift of miracles, gifts of healing, gift of helps/service, gift of administration/government/leadership, gift of tongues, gift of interpretation)

God's Prioritizing of Gifts

Now you are the body of Christ, and each one of you is a part of it. And in the church God has appointed first of all apostles, second prophets, third teachers, then workers of miracles, also those having gifts of healing, those able to help others, those with gifts of administration, and those speaking in different kinds of tongues. Are all apostles? Are all prophets? Are all teachers? Do all work miracles? Do all have gifts of healing? Do all speak in tongues? Do all interpret? But eagerly desire the greater gifts.

Romans 12

(gift of prophecy, gift of helps/service, gift of teaching, gift of exhortation/ encouragement, gift of giving, gift of administration/government/leadership, gift of showing mercy)

Living Sacrifices

Therefore, I urge you, brothers, in view of God's mercy, to offer your bodies as living sacrifices, holy and pleasing to God - this is your spiritual act of worship. Do not conform any longer to the pattern of this world, but be transformed by the renewing of your mind. Then you will be able to test and approve what God's will is - his good, pleasing, and perfect will.

Using Gifts According to Your Faith

For by the grace given me I say to every one of you: Do not think of yourself more highly than you ought, but rather think of yourself with sober judgment, in accordance with the measure of faith God has given you. Just as each of us has one body with many members, and these members do not all have the same function, so in Christ we who are many form one body, and each member belongs to all the others. We have different gifts, according to the grace given us. If a man's gift is prophesying, let him use it in proportion to his faith. If it is serving, let him serve; if it is teaching, let him teach; if it is encouraging, let him encourage; if it is contributing to the needs of others, let him give generously; if it is leadership, let him govern diligently; if it showing mercy, let him do it cheerfully.

The Fruit of Love

Love must be sincere. Hate what is evil; cling to what is good. Be devoted to one another in brotherly love. Honor one another above yourselves. Never be lacking in zeal, but keep your spiritual fervor, serving the Lord. Be joyful in hope, patient in affliction, faithful in prayer. Share with God's people who are in need. Practice hospitality.

Bless those who persecute you; bless and do not curse. Rejoice with those who rejoice; mourn with those who mourn. Live in harmony with one another. Do not be proud, but be willing to associate with people of low position. Do not be conceited.

Ephesians 4:7-13

(apostolic gift, prophetic gift, evangelistic gift, pastoral gift, teaching gift)

But to each one of us grace has been given as Christ apportioned it. This is why it says:

> "When he ascended on high, he led captives in his train and gave gifts to men."

(What does "he ascended" mean except that he also descended to the lower, earthly regions? He who descended is the very one who ascended higher than all the heavens, in order to fill the whole universe.) It was he who gave some to be apostles, some to be prophets, some to be evangelists, and some to be pastors and teachers, to prepare God's people for works of service, so that the body of Christ may be built up.

Ephesians 4:13-16

Gifts Give Maturity to the Body.

Until we all reach unity in the faith and in the knowledge of the Son of God and become mature, attaining to the whole measure of the fullness of Christ. Then we will no longer be infants, tossed back and forth by the waves, and blown here and there by every wind of teaching and by cunning and craftiness of men in their deceitful scheming. Instead, speaking the truth in love, we will in all things grow up into him who is the Head, that is, Christ. From him the whole body, joined and held together by every supporting ligament, grows and builds itself up in love, as each part does its work.

Additional Scriptures

Other Scriptures that deal with the Biblical gifts in the New Testament include:

1 Thessalonians 5:16-22

Importance of Prophecies

Be joyful always; pray continually; give thanks in all circumstances, for this is God's will for you in Christ Jesus. Do not put out the Spirit's fire; do not treat prophecies with contempt. Test everything. Hold on to the good. Avoid every kind of evil.

1 Peter 4:10,11

Speak as if God Is Speaking Through You.

Each one should use whatever gift he has received to serve others, faithfully administering God's grace in its various forms. If anyone speaks, he should do it as one speaking the very words of God. If anyone serves, he should do it with the strength God provides, so that in all things God may be praised through Jesus Christ. To him be the glory and the power for ever and ever. Amen.

1 Timothy 4:12-16

Do Not Neglect the Spiritual Gift Within You.

Don't let anyone look down on you because you are young, but set an example for the believers in speech, in life, in love, in faith and in purity. Until I come, devote yourself to the public reading of Scripture, to preaching and to teaching. Do not neglect your gift, which was given you through a prophetic message when the body of elders laid their hands on you. Be diligent in these matters; give yourself wholly to them, so that everyone may see your progress. Watch your life and doctrine closely. Persevere in them, because if you do, you will save both yourself and your hearers.

2 Timothy 1:6

Stir Up the Gift You Have.

For this reason I remind you to fan into flame the gift of God, which is in you through the laying on of my hands.

How to Classify the Biblical Gifts

Many authors have tried to put the gifts in some type of order. The following is an example.

Sample Lists of Classifying the Gifts

The following authors have classified the gifts into different lists or categories. These lists are representative of the broad spectrum within Christian circles including both Pentecostal-Charismatic and non-Pentecostal authors. We will give the author, then his classification of the gifts, and finally, we will give a brief explanation about the author.

J. Rodman Williams

Classification of Spiritual Gifts[2]

Gifts of Christ	**Gifts of God's Grace**		**Gifts of the Holy Spirit**
Domata	*Charismata*		*Spiritual Charismata*
Ephesians 4:11-12	Romans 12:6-8	1 Peter 4:10-11	1 Corinthians 12:8-10
Equipping Gifts	**Functional**	**Stewardship**	**Manifestation Gifts**
Apostles	Prophecy	Speaking	Word of Wisdom
Prophets	Serving	Serving	Word of Knowledge
Evangelists	Teaching		Faith
Pastors	Exhorting		Gifts of Healing
Teachers	Giving		Working of Miracles
	Leading		Prophecy
	Showing Mercy		Distinguishing of Spirits
			Kinds of Tongues
			Interpretation of Tongues

J. Rodman Williams is a professor of theology at Regent University. He has written a number of books including: *The Era of the Spirit, The Pentecostal Reality, The Gifts of the Holy Spirit Today*, and three volumes of *Renewal Theology.*

Leslie B. Flynn

Ministering Gifts[3]

Speaking	**Serving**	**Signifying**
1 Peter 4:11		2 Corinthians 12:12; Hebrew 2:3,4
Apostleship	Ministration (helps)	Miracles
Prophecy	Hospitality	Healings
Evangelism	Giving	Tongues
Pastoring	Government (ruling)	Interpretation
Teaching	Showing Mercy	
Exhorting	Faith	
Word of Wisdom	Discernment	
Word of Knowledge	Miracles	
Tongues	Healings	
Interpretation		

Leslie B. Flynn is the Instructor of Journalism at Nyack Missionary College and pastors the Grace Conservative Baptist Church, Nanuet, New York. He has authored: *Me Like Jesus?, Now A Word From Our Creator — The Ten Commandments Today, Great Church Fights,* and *19 Gifts of the Spirit: Which Do You Have? Are You Using Them?*

Marilyn Hickey

Three Major Divisions of Gifts[4]

Ministries	**Motive Gifts**	**Charismatic Gifts**	
Ephesians 4:11-12	Romans 12	1 Corinthians 12	
Apostle	Prophecy	Spoken:	Diverse Tongues
Prophet	Serving		Interpretation
Evangelist	Teaching		Prophecy
Pastor	Exhortation	Power:	Miracles
Teacher	Giving		Faith
	Organization		Healing
	Mercy	Revelation:	Knowledge
			Wisdom

Marilyn Hickey is the radio and television Bible teacher of the program, *Life for Laymen*, headquartered in Denver, Colorado.

David Pytches

Four Main Listings of Gifts[5]

Manifestations of the Spirit 1 Corinthians 12:8-10	**Ministries of the Spirit** 1 Corinthians 12:28	**Charismatic Gifts of Grace** Romans 12:3-8	**Equippers of the Saints** Ephesians 4:8-14	**Misc.** 1 Corinthians 7:7-8
Revelation:				
Word of wisdom	Apostles	Prophecy	Apostles	Celibacy
Word of knowledge	Prophets	Serving	Prophets	
Discerning of spirits	Teachers	Teaching	Evangelists	1 Corinthians 13:3
	Miracles	Exhortation	Pastors/Teachers	Philanthropy
	Gifts of healing	Giving		
Power:		Organizing		1 Peter 4:9
Gift of faith	Helps	Mercy		Hospitality
Gift of healing	Administration			
Working of miracles	Tongues			
Communications:				
Gifts of prophecy				
Kinds of tongues				
Interpretation of tongues				

David Pytches is an international Anglican renewal teacher and the vicar of Saint Andrew's, Chorleywood, Herts, England. Since 1983 he has served as an international director of the Sharing of Ministries Abroad. His book, *Spiritual Gifts in the Local Church*, has almost acquired textbook status among Anglican charismatics.

W.T. Purkiser

Purkiser's Listing of Gifts[6]

General Gifts Romans, 1 & 2 Corinthians		**Service Gifts** Romans 12:6-8, 1 Corinthians 12:7-11	
Justification	Romans 5:15-16	Prophesying	Ability to speak with wisdom
Eternal life	Romans 6:23	Serving	Ability to speak with knowledge
Apostle's ministry	Romans 1:11	Teaching	Faith
God's mercy	Romans 11:29	Encouraging	Healings
Life's station	1 Corinthians 7:7	Contributing	Miraculous Powers
Answered prayer	2 Corinthians 1:11	Leadership	Ability to distinguish between spirits
		Compassion	Different languages
			Interpretation of languages

W. T. Purkiser, the editor of *The Herald of Holiness*, the official magazine of the Church of the Nazarene, and a professor of theology in their seminary.

R.M. Riggs

Official List (1 Corinthians 12)[7]

Revelation	**Power**	**Utterance**
Word of Wisdom	Faith	Prophecy
Word of Knowledge	Miracles	Tongues
Discerning of Spirits	Healing	Interpretation

Supplemental (Romans 12:6)

- Teaching + Exhortation is a *blend of* prophecy, wisdom, and knowledge.
- Ministering, ruling, giving, and showing mercy is a ***blend of*** wisdom and power.

Ralph M. Riggs is an Assembly of God pastor, missionary, educator, administrator, and author of *The Spirit Himself* and *The Spirit-Filled Pastor's Guide*.

Harold Horton

Nine Spiritual Gifts (1 Corinthians 12)[8]

Gifts of Revelation	**Gifts of Power**	**Gifts of Inspiration**
A Word of Wisdom	Faith	Prophecy
A Word of Knowledge	Workings of Miracles	Divers Kinds of Tongues
Discerning of Spirits	Gifts of Healing	Interpretation of Tongues

Harold Horton was a British Pentecostal educator who taught most of his life at AGGBI Bible School. He became a prolific author and contributor to most English-language Pentecostal periodicals.

Raymond W. Hurn

Five Groups of Gifts[9]

Facilitating Gifts	**Ministering Gifts**	**Sign Gifts**	**Communication Gifts**	**Church Growth**
Romans 12	Romans 12 Ephesians 4	1 Corinthians 12	Romans 12 Corinthians 12	Ephesians 4
Leadership	Serving	Faith	Prophecy	Evangelist
Administration	Encouraging	Healing	Wisdom	Apostle
Teaching	Mercy	Miracles	Knowledge	
Giving	Helping	Discernment of Spirits	Languages	
	Pastoral Care		Interpretation of Languages	

Raymond W. Hurn, the executive director of Home Missions for the Church of the Nazarene and author of *The Spiritual Gifts Workshop* and *Finding Your Ministry: A Study of the Fruit and Gifts of the Spirit.*

The Most Recognized Classification

The following lists make some distinctions that many other lists omit. First, gifts are not all classified together as Gifts of the Holy Spirit. The Gifts of Christ in Ephesians 4 are different from the Gifts of the Holy Spirit, and the Charismatic Gifts are broken down into two different sections — the functional or motivational gifts from God the Father in Romans 12, and the manifestation gifts from the Holy Spirit in 1 Corinthians 12. Finally, a difference is made between spiritual gifts and natural talents.

Natural abilities or talents, such as music, crafts, or celibacy, are given to an individual at his natural birth, and are to be developed if they are to mature. These talents are Gifts of God (1 Timothy 4:4-5; James 1:17) that are given to believers and unbelievers alike for the benefit of the whole creation. Spiritual gifts, however, are supernatural gifts given as a direct result of spiritual birth and the presence of the Holy Spirit in the life of the believer.

One should also differentiate between gifts and the general callings and fruit of the Holy Spirit. All Christians are called, for instance, to pray, witness, be hospitable, love their fellow man, and to bear the fruit of the Spirit, i.e., love, joy, peace, etc. (Galatians 5:22-23).

MOST RECOGNIZED CLASSIFICATION

Gifts of Christ	**Functional Gifts**	**Gifts of the Holy Spirit**	**Gifts Prioritized By God**	**Gifts of God**
Equipping Gifts	**Motivational Gifts**	**(Spiritual Charismata)**	**God-Appointed**	**(all talents)**[10]
Ascension Gifts		**Manifestation Gifts**		
5-Fold Ministry Gifts				
Ministry Gifts				
Domata	*Charismata*	*Charismata*		
Ephesians 4:11-12	Romans 12:6-8	1 Corinthians 12:8-10	1 Corinthians 12:27-30	James 1:17
Apostles	Prophecy	Word of Wisdom	Apostles	Any natural talent given to human beings regardless of their spiritual condition
Prophets	Serving	Word of Knowledge	Prophets	
Evangelists	Teaching	Faith	Teachers	
Pastors	Exhorting	Gifts of Healing	Miracles	
Teachers	Giving	Working of Miracles[11]	Gifts of Healing	
	Leading	Prophecy	Helps	
	Showing Mercy	Distinguishing of Spirits	Administration	
		Kinds of Tongues	Kinds of Tongues	
		Interpretation of Tongues	Interpretation of Tongues	

Understanding the Classification

I. Gifts in the first column

A. The most common titles

The titles given to the gifts in the first column are listed on the top of the column: Gifts of Christ, Equipping Gifts, Ascension Gifts, 5-Fold Ministry Gifts, Ministry Gifts.

1. Gifts of Christ:

Gifts of Christ means these are the gifts Jesus Christ promised to give to the church. They are not promised from God the Father, nor from the Holy Spirit. They have come from Christ. The writer of Ephesians makes it clear that when Jesus ascended, He gave these gifts to the Church:

> When he ascended on high, he led captives in his train and gave gifts to men. (4:8)

Some have argued that Jesus left these gifts, often called offices, to the church to replace what He as one person did while He was on earth. In other words, He has left behind apostles, prophets, evangelists, pastors and teachers to do what He could do all by Himself. Jesus was all of these, but no man can be all of these. 1 Corinthians 12:28-31 helps us understand that not all are apostles, not all are prophets, teachers, etc. Ephesians 4:11,12 makes it clear that only "some" will be apostles and "some" will be prophets.

2. Equipping Gifts:

Equipping Gifts means that Jesus left these gifts to equip the saints or the Church. Ephesians 4:11 says,

> It was he who gave some to be apostles, some to be prophets, some to be evangelists, and some to be pastors and teachers, to prepare [equip, KJV] God's people for works of service....

In other words the apostle, prophet, evangelist, pastor and teacher were given to the Church to prepare, equip, and train the saints for works of service. It is important to note here that these offices or gifts are given to equip the saints, not to do it all themselves. They are the trainers, not the doers. Many churches hire "pastors" to do it all, not to train all.

3. Ascension Gifts:

Ascension Gifts is the title some give to this list because it emphasizes when this gift came into existence. This same passage in Ephesians says, "When he ascended on high . . . he gave gifts unto men." This means that Jesus gave these gifts to the Church when He ascended from the earth, after His death on Calvary and after the time of His resurrection. This means these gifts were given after Calvary. Why is this so important? Because it means the apostles and prophets appointed or in existence before His resurrection are not part of this gifting process. If they were, then this gifting was given to them after the Cross, and was given for the purpose of training the saints for works of service. For this reason it has been argued that the first post-ascension apostle fulfilling this office was Paul. Matthias, chosen to take Judas' place, had different qualifications for being one of the Twelve. He had to be a witness of all Jesus did and taught, and so was required to have been in company with Jesus from the time of Jesus' baptism to His resurrection.

> "Therefore it is necessary to choose one of the men who have been with us the whole time the Lord Jesus went in and out among us, beginning from John's baptism to the time when Jesus was taken up from us. For one of these must become a witness with us of his resurrection." So they proposed two men: Joseph called Barsabbas (also known as Justus) and Matthias.
>
> Acts 1:21-23

This scripture also tells us the role the 12 apostles expected to play, a role differing from the equipping/training role of the apostle given in Ephesians 4. Some have argued that all apostles died when

Jesus' apostles died, but the post-Ascension apostles of Ephesians 4 are to exist "until we all reach the unity in the faith and in the knowledge of the Son of God and become mature, attaining the whole measure of the fullness of Christ" (4:13) — and this will only happen when Jesus Christ returns. The apostle, prophet, evangelist, pastor, and teacher in Ephesians 4 are post-Ascension gifts given to train and equip the saints until Jesus returns. This is why Conner meticulously points out that there are 14 other post-Ascension apostles listed in Acts through Revelation other than the 12 disciples.[12]

4. Five-Fold Ministry Gifts

The *Five-Fold Ministry Gifts* is so called because there are five gifts mentioned. Many theologians propose that there are only four. They suggest that "pastor and teacher" is really one gift with a double-barreled title. This argument is derived from the Greek "article-noun-kai-noun" rule. However, Wallaby has just as adequately argued that the "article-noun-kai-noun" rule doesn't apply here.[13] It really isn't important if it is Four-Fold or Five-Fold; we must just remember that such a gift list was given by Christ to equip the church. Another writer has suggested a Seven-Fold ministry gifting. Included in his list are elders and deacons. However, Ephesians doesn't mention these two as gifts from Jesus in the same way it does the other five. From the studies we have compared, our preference is for a Five-Fold ministry.

5. Ministry Gifts

Ministry Gifts is the final common title given to this classification of gifts. It simply means these are gifts given to allow ministry to take place. The Five-Fold are to train the Church for ministry. In one sense it is a misnomer because *all gifts are given for ministry in one form or another.* The Five-Fold are not the only ministry gifts.

B. The Scriptures

Ephesians 4:8-12 is the basis for the use of these gifts in this manner.

C. The Greek Usage

Domata is the Greek word for this gift.

The *domata* of Ephesians 4 represent offices. They include "prophets" ("He gave some . . . as prophets" [v.11 NASB]) who hold a continuing office in the church. Prophecy in 1 Corinthians 12:10 is an activity not limited to the office.[14]

D. The List of Leadership Gifts According to Ephesians 4:8-12

Following the above information we have simply listed each gift mentioned under this classification. Definitions and usage of each gift are handled separately and later on in the workbook.

1. Apostolic Gift
2. Prophetic Gift
3. Evangelistic Gift
4. Pastoral/Shepherding Gift
5. Teaching Gift

II. Gifts in the Second Column

A. The most common titles

The titles given to these gifts, i.e., the Functional Gifts or the Motivational Gifts, are most commonly given to the list of gifts in Romans 12. While Paul does not say that these gifts in this chapter in Romans are given by the Holy Spirit, he follows his argument about the power of the Holy Spirit (ch. 8), and it is given in the same format as 1 Corinthians 12-14. In the Corinthian passage he gives an illustration of the different gifts in the body of Christ as representing different parts in the body. This is the same type of argument he uses here for these gifts. The Greek word for gifts, *charismata*, is the same word used in 1 Corinthians 12 and Romans 12. Therefore, it is the opinion of some that the functional or motivational gifts are definitely gifts given supernaturally by the Holy Spirit.[15] However, the context seems to attribute these functional gifts to God. In Romans 12:1 and all the way through the passage there is no mention of the Holy Spirit like Paul discusses in 1 Corinthians 12-14. It is our understanding that these functional gifts are the gifts from God the Father so that all three parts of the Godhead present gifts to the church. Jesus, in Ephesians 4, gives the church the Equipping gifts; the Holy Spirit gives the manifestational gifts in 1 Corinthians 12-14; and here in Romans 12, the Father gives the Functional gifts.

1. Functional Gifts:

The gifts are called Functional Gifts because Paul says that all these gifts do not have the same function. Just as each member of the human body has a particular function to perform, so it is that each member of Christ's body has supernatural gifts.

> Prior to Paul's listing these seven gifts, he writes: "For as in one body we have many members, and all the members do not have the same function [f.n. The Greek word *praxin*, a form of *praxis* ("acting, activity, function" —-BAGD). Cf. our English word *praxis*. The KJV translation as "office" is less adequate than "function" or "activity."] so we, though many, are one body in Christ, and individually members one of another" (Romans 12:4-5). As each member of the human body has a particular function to fulfill, so it is with each member of the body of Christ.[16]

2. Motivational Gifts:

A Motivational Gift is a particular gift which God gives to each Christian that motivates his life, so that when the Christian spiritually discerns this gift, he leaves the arena of insecurity and knows his position of ministry in life.[17]

B. The Scriptures

Romans 12:6-8 is the basis for the use of these gifts in this manner.

C. The Greek Usage

Charismata is the Greek word for these gifts. It means "gifts of grace." It is a term for a gift in reference to the service of others in the community. The word *charisma* is used to refer to a wide range of gifts. However, in all their variety each gift represents God's gracious bestowal. Thayer defines *charisma* as "a gift of grace; a favor which one receives without any merit of his own." The gifts are, and remain, gifts of God's grace.[18]

D. The List of Gifts

1. Gift of Prophecy
2. Gift of Helps/Service
3. Gift of Teaching
4. Gift of Exhortation/Encouragement
5. Gift of Giving
6. Gift of Administration/Government/Leadership
7. Gift of Showing Mercy

III. Gifts in the Third Column

A. The most common titles

The titles given to the gifts in the third column are listed on the top of the column: Gifts of the Holy Spirit, Spiritual Charismata, and Manifestation Gifts.

1. Gifts of the Holy Spirit

Gifts of the Holy Spirit means that these gifts are given to members of the body of Christ by the Holy Spirit, "just as he determines" [v.11]. That these are gifts given by the Holy Spirit is emphasized several times throughout 1 Corinthians 12:7-11:

v. 7 "of the Spirit"
v. 8 "through the Spirit . . . by means of the same Spirit"
v. 9 "by the same Spirit . . . by that one Spirit"
v.11 "All these are the work of one and the same Spirit . . . . "

2. Spiritual Charismata

The Greek word for gifts used in this passage is *charismata.* Thus, these are spiritual "gifts of grace," or Spiritual Charismata.

3. Manifestation Gifts

Manifestation Gifts means that these gifts are manifestations of the Holy Spirit:

> Now to each one the manifestation of the Spirit is given for the common good. (1 Corinthians 12:7)

B. The Scriptures

1 Corinthians 12:7-11 is the basis for the use of these gifts in this manner.

C. The Greek Usage

Charismata is the Greek word for these gifts. See discussion in previous section for explanation of the term.

D. The List of Gifts

1. Word of Wisdom
2. Word of Knowledge
3. Gift of Faith
4. Gifts of Healing
5. Gift of Miracles
6. Gift of Prophecy
7. Gift of Discernment of Spirits
8. Gift of Tongues
9. Gift of Interpretation

IV. Gifts in the Fourth Column

A. The most common titles

The titles given to the gifts in the fourth column are listed on the top of the column: Gifts Prioritized by God and God-Appointed Gifts.

1. Gifts Prioritized by God

   Gifts Prioritized by God is a title given to this list of gifts because the gifts have been listed by God, according to Paul, in order of priority in this particular passage of scripture.

2. God-Appointed

   God-Appointed is the title given to these gifts, according to 1 Corinthians 12:28: "God has appointed...."

B. The Scriptures

1 Corinthians 12:27-28 is where these gifts are found. However, the Greek word for gifts used in this passage is not emphasized. Instead, emphasis is given to the organizational order of these gifts.

C. The Greek Usage

Charismata is the Greek word for these gifts. See the discussion on *charismata* in Section II for a description of the term.

D. The List of Gifts

1. Apostolic Gift
2. Prophetic Gift
3. Teaching Gift
4. Gift of Miracles
5. Gifts of Healing
6. Gift of Helps/Service
7. Gift of Administration/Government/Leadership
8. Gift of Tongues
9. Gift of Interpretation

V. Gifts in the Fifth Column

A. The most common titles

The titles given to the gifts in the fifth column are listed on the top of the column: Gifts of God — Talents.

These gifts are not gifts of the Spirit. An unregenerate man has the same talents as a regenerated Spirit-filled man. All people receive these gifts from God. They can be developed and improved by home environment and training. The talents differ from the spiritual gifts (supernaturally endowed), but are more likely to flow as the person matures in his/her faith. This is why Peter urges us to use whatever gifts we have (1 Peter 4:10,11).

B. The Scriptures

We have chosen the scripture reference for this category as James 1:17.

C. The Greek Usage

No Greek usage for these gifts is given, as each talent has a different word and should be studied individually.

D. The List of Talents

1. Art
2. Music
3. Drama
4. Sports
5. Celibacy
6. Poverty
7. Martyrdom
8. *Ad infinitum* (without end or limit)

(c.f. note 10, p.178)

The Gifts of Christ — The Equipping Gifts

The following material deals with the gifts that have been listed in the first column, "Most Recognized Classification" — Gifts of Christ. Each gift has been listed separately, along with the corresponding scriptural references. Also given is the Greek usage for each gift. The corresponding number from *Strong's Exhaustive Concordance* is noted to help those who are not Greek scholars (e.g. sc4396).

We then have quoted definitions from scholars from various persuasions who have written on the subject, followed by our suggested definition. Finally, we have listed strengths and weaknesses of these gifts.

MOST RECOGNIZED CLASSIFICATION

Gifts of Christ	**Functional Gifts**	**Gifts of the Holy Spirit**	**Gifts Prioritized By God**	**Gifts of God**
Equipping Gifts	**Motivational Gifts**	**(Spiritual Charismata)**	**God-Appointed**	**(all talents)**
Ascension Gifts		**Manifestation Gifts**		
5-Fold Ministry Gifts				
Ministry Gifts				
Domata	*Charismata*	*Charismata*		
Ephesians 4:11-12	Romans 12:6-8	1 Corinthians 12:8-10	1 Corinthians 12:27-30	James 1:17
Apostles	Prophecy	Word of Wisdom	Apostles	
Prophets	Serving	Word of Knowledge	Prophets	
Evangelists	Teaching	Faith	Teachers	
Pastors	Exhorting	Gifts of Healing	Miracles	
Teachers	Giving	Working of Miracles	Gifts of Healing	
	Leading	Prophecy	Helps	
	Showing Mercy	Distinguishing of Spirits	Administration	
		Kinds of Tongues	Kinds of Tongues	
		Interpretation of Tongues	Interpretation of Tongues	

1. Apostolic Leadership Gift

Scriptures: Ephesians 4:11-12; 1 Corinthians 12:28

Greek Usage: *apostolos* (SC652) One who is sent forth with authority.

Various Definitions:

Bruce L. Bugbee: The divine enablement to start churches and oversee their development.[19]

Kevin Conner: One sent as a messenger, the bearer of a commission, Church planter, spiritual father of Churches.[20]

Frank Damazio: One sent forth with orders; a delegate or ambassador; bearer of a commission.[21]

Leslie B. Flynn: The missionary gift[22] is the continuing aspect of the apostleship. 1) sent 2) cross-culturally with 3) church planting goals.[23]

Donald Gee: The great importance of the work involved in true apostleship means far more than being "the Lord's messenger-boy": it is an office clothed with dignity and power, always first on the list of God-given ministers. The Apostle is sent by Christ in the same way that He was sent by the Father; and with at least something of all that that implies of authority and power, and of grace and love.[24]

Howard Snyder: The word "apostle" or "apostles" occurs eighty-one times in the New Testament. A survey of this usage will shed light on a proper biblical definition.

1. The apostles were the twelve disciples chosen by Jesus. This meaning appears seven times in the Gospels, as well as in Acts 1:2 and possibly Jude 17.
2. The term designates the principal leaders of the early church in the book of Acts. In Acts 1, Matthias was chosen to replace Judas and was added to the eleven apostles (Acts 1:26). This usage, the original eleven plus Matthias, occurs 14 times in Acts 1 through 6.
3. Beginning with Acts 8, the term is expanded to include other emerging leaders. Paul and Barnabas (Acts 14:4, 14), Jesus' brother James (Galatians 1:19), Apollos (1 Corinthians 4:9), Silas (1 Thessalonians 2:7) and Andronicus and Junias (Romans 16:7). This particular usage in Acts appears 24 times . . . . [25]

B. E. Underwood: This is the person with the special ability to provide authoritative leadership for a cluster of churches. This often involves the founding of churches, but may also focus on giving new direction to the churches.[26]

C. Peter Wagner: The special ability that God gives to certain members of the body of Christ to assume and exercise general leadership over a number of churches with an extraordinary authority in spiritual matters that is spontaneously recognized and appreciated by those churches.[27]

Suggested Definition:

The special supernatural Ascension Gift, differing from the 12 apostles (pre-Ascension), that God gives to certain members of the body of Christ to assume and exercise general leadership over and equip the Church with an extraordinary authority in spiritual matters. The Apostolic gift that is active in the church today is one that is manifested in people who have been given a spiritual authority to gather others in the work of the Lord, normally to start churches or establish order in or build existing ones.

Good Biblical Example: Paul

Suggested Characteristics:

1. Will have *spiritual authority* from God in order to guide workers in their service of the Lord (Acts 16:1-4,9,10; 17:15; 20:3-5,13,14; 1 Corinthians 16:10-12; 8:6; 2 Corinthians 8:16-18).
2. Is willing to *devote his life* to planting and establishing the church (1 Thessalonians 2:7).
3. Will be involved in *founding and/or establishing* churches, programs or ministries (1 Corinthians 5:1-13; 2 Corinthians 2:6-11).
4. Will preach and teach the Word (1 Timothy 2:7; 2 Timothy 1:11).
5. Will prepare, ordain, and appoint other ministries (Acts 6:1-6; 16:1-4).
6. Will be involved in implementing Church discipline (Matthew 18:15-17; 1 Corinthians 4:21; Acts 15; 2 Thessalonians 3:14).
7. Will have a vision for the whole body of Christ (Ephesians 3:1-9; 4:1-16).
8. Will organize God's house in Divine order (1 Corinthians 11:34; 7:17; 16:1-2).
9. May have a sense of calling to a particular people or group (Galatians 2:8).
10. Will tend to form teams that will work with him (Acts 16:9; 18:2-24; 19:24).
11. Senses God's direction for the Church.

12. Has a burden for the Church universally (2 Corinthians 11:28).
13. Is more concerned for God's plan than individual needs.
14. Focuses on spiritual growth of groups more than of individuals.

Suggested Potential Weaknesses:

1. Lacks ability to concentrate long on one area; lacks longevity.
2. Is program- rather than people-oriented.
3. Lacks one-on-one ability.
4. Tends to be authoritarian.

2. Prophetic Leadership Gift

Scriptures: 1 Corinthians 12:28, 29; Ephesians 4:11-12

Greek Usage: *prophetees* (SC4396) To foretell events; speak under divine inspiration; to proclaim a divine revelation or speak forth an inspired message.

Various Definitions:

Kevin J. Conner: A spokesman for another, an interpreter for God, a seer, a divinely commissioned and inspired person, a foreteller of the future gifted for the exposition of the truth.[28]

Frank Damazio: Foreteller of God's Word and future events; forthteller of God's Word under inspiration of the Spirit; mouthpiece or spokesman for God; an interpreter of God's Word.[29]

Hobart Freeman: The prophets were the teachers of true religion, but interwoven in their ethical preaching were to be found numerous predictions of future events as well as warnings against the dangers of religious apostasy (Isaiah 52; 58; Ezekiel 3:17; 33:7).[30]

B. E. Underwood: This is that gifted person who has the supernatural ability to interpret the Scriptures in light of the present situation in the church. The prophetic gift is correcting, encouraging and edifying.[31]

Suggested Definition:

The special supernatural Ascension Gift differing from the pre-Ascension prophets that God gives to certain members of the body of Christ to represent God before the Church as a spokesman and equipping agent, to present the heart, will, and purpose of God in forthtelling or foretelling.

Good Biblical Example: Agabus in Acts

Suggested Characteristics:

1. Has strong desire to speak forth the truth, especially as it pertains to right and wrong, good and evil; will include exhortation, reproof, warning, edification, and comfort (Acts 15:32; 1 Corinthians 14:3; Ephesians 5:11; Jeremiah 20:9).
2. Is concerned for reputation of God and the fulfillment of His program (John 2:13-17).
3. Has a strong vision for what God wants to do and declares it clearly to men (Ephesians 3:1-5).
4. Is extremely bold; does not mince words (Luke 3:7ff; Galatians 2:11ff).
5. Focuses on spiritual growth of groups more than individuals; has a concern for the corporate holiness of God's people, desiring them to be truly set apart by their lifestyle, values, and relationships (Matthew 5-7; Revelation 2-3).
6. Confirms direction (Acts 13:1-3).
7. Has an integral part in establishing the foundations of the Church (Ephesians 2:20-22).
8. Experiences much brokenness in his life; identifies with the sins and failings of God's people (Isaiah 22:4; Jeremiah 4:19; 8:21ff).
9. His life is characterized by great spiritual intensity and discipline; spends much time in prayer and fasting (Luke 2:26-37).
10. Often uses the gifts of the Word of Knowledge and Word of Wisdom (Acts 21:10-11).
11. May have a desire to write down the declarations of God's heart (1 Thessalonians. 5:19-20).
12. On occasions can predict national events as well as personal destinies (Acts 5:1-11; 11:27-30; 21:8-14).
13. Often suffers rejection because of his word and is not duly honored (Matthew 13:57; 23:34; Luke 4:24; Revelation 11).
14. Has a life calling to ministering to the body of Christ.

Suggested Potential Weaknesses:

1. Tends to be judgmental and blunt, and dwells on the negative (Jonah 3:4).
2. Frankness may be viewed as harshness (Galatians 1:6-9; 5:7-12).
3. Tends to condemn self when there is failure to evoke the right response in others (Jeremiah 20:7-18).
4. Tends to take on responsibility which is not rightfully his own (Romans 14:4).
5. If self is too strong (pride) and there is a lack of sober self-assessment (humility, purity), the danger is great to be deceived and to deceive others in turn (Jeremiah 23; Ezekiel 13; 2 Peter 2).
6. Because of tendency to be excessively critical, needs to consciously develop attitudes of mercy and patience (Romans 9:1-3; 1 Thessalonians 5:14).
7. Neither his utterances nor his writings are to be considered as normative or infallible; his words must be judged by the Word of God (1 Corinthians 14:29,30).
8. His manner of expression is very authoritative and at times even negative (Acts 21:10-12; 2 Corinthians 13:2-3; 1 Thessalonians 4:8).

3. Evangelistic Leadership Gift

Scriptures: Ephesians 4:11-12

Greek Usage: *euaggelistes* (SC2099) A preacher of the gospel; to announce the good news; to declare, bring, good tidings.

Various Definitions:

Bruce L. Bugbee: The divine enablement to effectively communicate the message of Christ to unbelievers so that they respond in faith and discipleship.[32]

Kevin J. Conner: One who announces glad tidings, one who enlarges and extends the kingdom of God, one who shares in edifying and building the Church.[33]

Frank Damazio: Preacher of the Gospel (messenger of good news); preacher having a harvesting ministry.[34]

Leslie B. Flynn: The gift of proclaiming the Good News of salvation effectively so that people respond to the claims of Christ in conversion and in discipleship.[35]

B. E. Underwood: An evangelist is that person with the ability to present the gospel in such a way that people will respond to the claims of Christ by repentance, conversion, and discipleship. The evangelist also has the ability to prepare others for their ministry of evangelizing.[36]

C. Peter Wagner: The special ability that God gives to certain members of the body of Christ to share the gospel with unbelievers in such a way that men and women become Jesus' disciples and responsible members of the body of Christ.[37]

Suggested Definition:

The special supernatural Ascension Gift that God gives to certain members of the body of Christ to both proclaim the Good News of salvation with extraordinary effectiveness and to equip God's people in their personal and corporate soul-winning efforts.

Good Biblical Example: Philip

Suggested Characteristics:

1. Enjoys talking about Jesus to the lost (Acts 8:5).
2. Is very instrumental in leading others to believe in Christ as Savior (2 Timothy 4:5).
3. Has a burden for the lost (Romans 9:1-3).
4. Enjoys being with unbelievers in order to share the gospel (Acts 8:25).
5. Is able to persuade people to make decisions (2 Corinthians 5:14-15).
6. Is able to sense when a person does not know Jesus Christ, and to have compassion for that person (Acts 8:34-35).
7. Feels a life calling into the evangelistic ministry.

Suggested Potential Weaknesses:

1. Is judgmental toward others who are not involved in evangelism (Luke 9:45-46).
2. Relies on own power of expression or persuasion to convert people (1 Corinthians 2:1-5).
3. Because emphasis is on winning the lost, could be viewed as lacking spiritual depth.

4. Pastoral/Shepherding Leadership Gift

Scriptures: Ephesians 4:11-12

Greek Usage: *poimen* (SC4166) A shepherd, one who tends herds or flocks (not merely one who feeds them) . . . . Pastors guide as well as feed the flock (Acts 20:28).[38] It is translated "shepherd" 17 times, and "pastor" once.

Various Definitions:

Bruce L. Bugbee: The divine enablement to lead, care for, and nurture individuals or groups in the body as they grow in their faith.[39]

Kevin J. Conner: One who tends the sheep, a shepherd, one who cares for the sheep. One who leads, feeds, waters and guards the sheep, guardian.[40]

Frank Damazio: Herdsman of God's people; an overseer of the Church; one who tends, guards, feeds, and guides the flock of God.[41]

Leslie B. Flynn: Helping to mature the saints with a view to their Christian service. Not surprisingly, a major aspect of the non-official gift of shepherding is helping others to discover their gifts and then guiding them into channels of ministry. 1) to guide 2) to graze 3) to guard. The Greek word for pastor comes from the verb "to feed" and is used 3 times in the New Testament to mean "providing food": John 21:16 — "feed my sheep"; Acts 20:28 — "feed the church of God"; 1 Peter 5:2 — "feed the flock of God."[42]

C. Peter Wagner: The gift of pastor is the special ability that God gives to certain members of the body of Christ to assume a long-term personal responsibility for the spiritual welfare of a group of believers.[43]

Suggested Definition:

The special supernatural Ascension Gift that God gives to certain members of the body of Christ to equip and care for the spiritual well-being of the flock of God.

Good Biblical Example: Timothy

Suggested Characteristics:

1. Assumes responsibility for tender care and vigilant superintendence.
2. Enjoys one-to-one discipling and caring.
3. Assumes responsibility when he sees a Christian being led astray.
4. Is able to watch over, guide, train, and nurture other believers toward spiritual maturity and work of the ministry.
5. Senses a shepherding (caring) instinct.
6. Enjoys training saints for the work of ministry.
7. Has personal experience of affliction — God comforts us that we may comfort others (2 Corinthians 1:4).
8. Has ability to give empathetic and undivided attention to someone in need — to set aside one's own interests and concerns in order to be more fully present to one who is suffering (Philippians 2:5-7).
9. Empathizes.
10. Shows vulnerability — "wounded healer."
11. Is able to maintain confidentiality.
12. Desires to comfort those who are ill or grieving and to help them find Christ as the center of their lives.
13. Desires to help others to be healed of past hurts through forgiveness and prayer.
14. Desires to help others resolve issues concerning belief, doubt, sin, guilt (true and false), and life's meaning.
15. Feels a call into full-time ministry of caring.

Suggested Potential Weaknesses:

1. Becomes overly involved with individuals at the expense of the group.
2. Tends to have narrow vision of local ministry rather than corporate.
3. May lack organizational abilities.
4. In an effort to disciple, neglects evangelism.
5. May foster dependency in the one being helped.
6. May feel powerless if unable to provide specific solutions to another's suffering.
7. May not discern another's need for more professional help with problems.

5. Teaching Gift

Scriptures: Ephesians 4:11-12; 1 Corinthians 12:28,29

Greek Usage: *didaskalos* (SC1320) An instructor — one who communicates content (truth), trains others in practical skills, and models a lifestyle. Often used in the gospels in reference to or in addressing Jesus (corresponding to the Hebraic title "rabbi"). Translated "Doctor," 14 times; "Master," 47 times; "Teacher," 10 times; "Scribe," 67 times; "Teacher of the Law." It occurs 58 times in the New Testament — 48 in the gospels, of which 41 refer to Jesus (29 in direct address).

Various Definitions:

Bruce L. Bugbee: One who has the divine enablement to understand, clearly explain, and apply the Word of God to the lives of listeners.[44]

Kevin J. Conner: One who instructs, the occupation of teaching, someone qualified to instruct others, someone who imparts Bible truth to others.[45]

Frank Damazio: Instructor in God's Word; one who imparts systematic knowledge; a teacher of other teachers.[46]

C. Peter Wagner: The gift of teaching is the special ability that God gives to certain members of the body of Christ to communicate information relevant to the health and ministry of the body and its members in such a way that others will learn.[47]

Suggested Definition:

The special supernatural Ascension Gift that God gives to certain members of the body of Christ to present God's Word in a manner that displays spiritual authority and unusual, accurate promoting of health and maturity, while equipping individual members and the body itself for the work of ministry.

Suggested Characteristics:

1. Tends to be systematic (Acts 20:20, 27).
2. Enjoys studying the Word and doing research (Ezra 7:10).
3. Is a good communicator (Acts 18:24-26).
4. Is responsible for teaching other teachers (2 Timothy 2:2).
5. Has a desire to teach, to pass on truth and information (Romans 1:11; Colossians 1:28,29).
6. Tends to be concerned with details; strives for accuracy of content and expression (Acts 17:11).
7. Tends to work well in teacher-student relationships (Luke 19:47,48; 21:37-38).
8. Tends to be orderly in presentation (Nehemiah 8:7-8).
9. Has a life calling to teaching the body of Christ.

Suggested Potential Weaknesses:

1. By reason of his ministry, appeals to reason, understanding, and logic, and may lack emotional appeal.
2. Tends toward being legalistic and dogmatic.
3. Shows too much concern about head knowledge and too little concern with heart knowledge.
4. Is more concerned about content of teaching than person being taught.
5. Gives the impression that he or she is the only source of faith.
6. May not live by his/her own teaching.
7. Has the ability to make the Word say whatever he/she wants it to say.
8. May teach certain doctrines to an extreme.
9. May not incorporate enough practical creativity in teaching, and therefore must fight dullness.
10. May become unteachable if pride gets in the way.

The Functional Gifts

The following material deals with the gifts that have been listed in the second column, "Most Recognized Classification" — The Functional Gifts. Each gift has been listed separately, along with the corresponding scriptural references. Also given is the Greek usage for each gift. The corresponding number from *Strong's Concordance* is noted to help those who are not Greek scholars (e.g., SC4396).

We then have quoted definitions from scholars from various persuasions who have written on the subject, followed by our suggested definition. Following this is recorded the little that various authors have said about characteristics of the strengths and weaknesses of these gifts. Finally, we have listed strengths and weaknesses of these gifts.

MOST RECOGNIZED CLASSIFICATION

Gifts of Christ	**Functional Gifts**	**Gifts of the Holy Spirit**	**Gifts Prioritized By God**	**Gifts of God**
Equipping Gifts	**Motivational Gifts**	**(Spiritual Charismata)**	**God-Appointed**	**(all talents)**
Ascension Gifts		**Manifestation Gifts**		
5-Fold Ministry Gifts				
Ministry Gifts				
Domata	*Charismata*	*Charismata*		
Ephesians 4:11-12	Romans 12:6-8	1 Corinthians 12:8-10	1 Corinthians 12:27-30	James 1:17
Apostles	Prophecy	Word of Wisdom	Apostles	
Prophets	Serving	Word of Knowledge	Prophets	
Evangelists	Teaching	Faith	Teachers	
Pastors	Exhorting	Gifts of Healing	Miracles	
Teachers	Giving	Working of Miracles	Gifts of Healing	
	Leading	Prophecy	Helps	
	Showing Mercy	Distinguishing of Spirits	Administration	
		Kinds of Tongues	Kinds of Tongues	
		Interpretation of Tongues	Interpretation of Tongues	

1. Gift of Prophecy

Scriptures: Romans 12:6-8

Greek Usage: *propheteia* (SC4393) Speaking forth the mind and counsel of God.

Various Definitions:

Bruce L. Bugbee: The divine enablement to proclaim God's truth with power and clarity in a timely and culturally sensitive fashion for correction, repentance or edification.[48]

Kevin Conner: He who prophesies, a gifted faculty of setting forth inspired utterance in known languages.[49]

Frank Damazio: To occasionally foretell future events; to speak under the inspiration of God's Spirit; a gifted member who inspires, confirms and reinforces revealed truth.[50]

Leslie B. Flynn: The Spirit-given ability to proclaim the written Word of God with clarity and to apply it to a particular situation with a view to correction or edification.[51]

Don and Katie Fortune: One who is especially sensitive to perceiving the will of God, and then proclaiming it — or, depending upon the Lord's direction, praying for it to be accomplished. The perceiver, then, is one who readily perceives, prays about, proclaims, and promotes the will of God.[52]

B. E. Underwood: Prophecy is the manifestation of a spontaneously uttered word from the Lord given through any member of the body for the encouragement, edification, or exhortation of the church. This is the one gift that is both a ministry and a manifestation.[53]

C. Peter Wagner: The special ability that God gives to certain members of the body of Christ to receive and communicate an immediate message of God to His people through a divinely-anointed utterance.[54]

Suggested Definition:

The supernatural Functional Gift that God gives to certain members of the body of Christ which enables them to act often as one in the office of a prophet, but without a life calling to be an ordained minister. They often receive and communicate a message from God to mankind through a divinely-anointed utterance. They have special spiritual insight. (This gift differs from the office of the Prophetic Leader mentioned in the Five Fold and from the Manifestation Gift of Prophecy.)

Good Biblical Example: Peter and John the Baptist

Various Characteristics and Potential Weaknesses:

Don and Katie Fortune[55]

Characteristics of the Perceiver:

1. Quickly and accurately identifies good and evil and hates evil.
2. Sees everything as either black or white; no gray or indefinite areas.
3. Easily perceives the character of individuals and groups.
4. Encourages repentance that produces good fruit.
5. Believes the acceptance of difficulties will produce positive personal brokenness.
6. Has only a few or no close friendships.
7. Views the Bible as the basis for truth, belief, action, and authority.
8. Boldly operates on spiritual principles.
9. Is frank, outspoken, and doesn't mince words.
10. Is very persuasive in method of speaking.
11. Grieves deeply over the sins of others.
12. Is eager to see his own blind spots and to help others see theirs too.
13. Desires above all else to see God's plan worked out in all situations.
14. Strongly promotes the spiritual growth of groups and individuals.
15. Is called to intercession.
16. Feels the need to verbalize or dramatize what he "sees."
17. Tends to be introspective.
18. Has strong opinions and convictions.
19. Has strict personal standards.
20. Desires to be obedient to God at all costs.

Problems of the Perceiver:

1. Tends to be judgmental and blunt.
2. Forgets to praise partial progress due to goal consciousness.
3. Is pushy in trying to get others and groups to mature spiritually.
4. Is intolerant of opinions and views that differ from his own.
5. Struggles with self-image problems.

Gothard[56]

Characteristics:

1. The need to *express* thoughts and ideas verbally, especially regarding right and wrong.
2. The tendency to make *quick judgments* on what is seen and heard, and to speak up quickly.
3. An amazing ability to sense when someone or something is not what it appears to be and to react harshly to dishonesty.
4. A desire to reject those who offend so that justice will be done and others will be warned.
5. An openness about personal faults and failures and an honesty about himself as well as others.
6. A tendency to be impulsive in actions and to be wholeheartedly involved in whatever is done.
7. A tendency to be painfully direct when correcting friends.
8. A desire to give open evidences of loyalty and total commitment.
9. A willingness to suffer for doing what is right.
10. An ability to be very persuasive in defining what is right and what is wrong.

How Prophets Can Misuse Their Gift:

1. Correcting people who are not their responsibility.
2. Jumping to conclusions about words, actions and motives.
3. Reinforcing a condemning spirit.

4. Judging and exposing an offender rather than restoring the offender.
5. Cutting off a person who has failed.
6. Dwelling on the negative rather than the positive.
7. Lacking cautiousness and tactfulness in expressing opinions.
8. Demanding a positive response to a harsh rebuke.
9. Condemning themselves when they fail.
10. Accusing others if they don't fully reveal faults.

Hickey[57]

Characteristics:

1. Need to express message verbally.
2. Ability to discern character and motives of people.
3. Capacity to identify, define, and hate evil.
4. Willingness to experience brokenness to prompt brokenness.
5. Dependence on Scriptural truth to validate authority.
6. Desire for outward evidences to demonstrate inward conviction.
7. Directness, frankness, and persuasiveness.
8. Concern for reputation and program of God.
9. Inward weeping and personal identification with sins of those he talks with.
10. Eagerness to have others point out their own blindspots so they can help others.

Misunderstandings:

1. Frankness may be viewed as harshness.
2. Interest in groups may be interpreted as disinterest in individuals.
3. Efforts to gain results may be seen as using gimmicks.
4. Focus on right and wrong may be judged as intolerance of partial good.
5. Emphasis on decisions may appear as neglecting spiritual growth.
6. Public boldness and strict standards may hinder intimate personal relationships.

7. The strong desire to convey truth may be interpreted as little interest in listening to another's view.

Practical Christian Living Class Notes (pp. 41, 42)

Characteristics:

1. Strong desire to speak forth the truth, especially as it pertains to right and wrong, good and evil. (Romans 12:9)
2. Tendency to make snap judgments and to respond quickly.
3. Ability to "see" true character and motive of others; spot dishonesty.
4. Tendency to reject those who continually sin out of concern for justice and to warn others.
5. Openness about personal sins and failures; an honesty about self as well as others.
6. Deep concern for the reputation and program of God even to the point of personal suffering.
7. Persuasiveness in defining right and wrong.
8. Tendency to be impulsive, impetuous, and wholehearted in thought and deed.
9. Willingness to be broken that others might be broken.
10. Tendency to be painfully direct when correcting others, even friends.
11. Strong dependency on the Bible to validate his sense of authority.
12. Desire to give open evidence of loyalty and commitment.
13. Look for immediate response (repentance).

In the Spirit	*In the Flesh*
Committed to truth	Highly deceptive
Number 1 priority is obedience to God	Rebelliousness, domineering
Deeply sincere	Hypocritical, manipulative
Pure, holy, virtuous	Sensuous, lustful
Extremely bold	Very fearful
Very forgiving	Reject others and feel their rejection
Very persuasive	Very argumentative

Potential Problems:

1. Frankness may be viewed as harshness.
2. Tendency to dwell on negative.
3. Strong desire to speak truth may be seen as intolerance.
4. Interest in groups may be interpreted as disinterest in individuals.
5. Emphasis on decisions may appear as neglecting spiritual growth.
6. Tendency to condemn self when there is a failure to evoke the right response in others.
7. Tendency to take on responsibility which is not rightfully their own.
8. Boldness and high standards may hinder intimate relationships with others.
9. Tendency toward projecting his own type of gift and ministry onto others.

Suggested Characteristics:

1. Has a burden to share God's Word to the body.
2. Harmonizes with God's own Word in Scripture (the same Spirit speaks). Never takes from nor adds to the Scriptures, but will intensify and quicken that which already has been given to us of God. Brings forth things new and old out of the Scriptures of truth and will make them living and powerful to us.
3. Builds up the community. The whole purpose is positive, although there may be admonition and warning, even exhortation, to desist from some evil. Has a real lifting power and gives real light on the truth to those who hear.
4. Finds consent and agreement in the minds and hearts of others in the community. There should be a prevailing sense in the community that the prophecy was divinely inspired.
5. May be spoken in a variety of ways as the Lord Himself wills it.
6. It comes forth in power of the Spirit of God.
7. Spontaneity marks such an occasion, and the words are divinely inspired.
8. The prophetic word should be given in an orderly manner (1 Corinthians 14:31-33).
9. Not infallible, and the utterance must be judged by the infallible Word of God. The person should be humble enough to allow his word to be judged (1 Corinthians 14:29). If it is the mind of God, there is nothing to fear.
10. Prophecy has a vital connection with faith; the individual must prophesy according to the measure of faith (Romans 12:6).
11. It stays on the sober ground of faith (cf. Romans 12:6). God gives, and the believer makes responsible use of the gifts. Prophecy declares God's counsel openly (1 Corinthians 14:5) and edifies the whole Church, although there may be exhortation and admonition and warning to desist from some evil (14:2-3).

Suggested Potential Weaknesses:

1. Deals with things that do not edify and are designed to puff up hearers and to lead them into error.
2. If you are not humble enough to allow your prophecy to be judged, it is as surely wrong as you are wrong.
3. If you hear any voices that make you think that you are superior to those whom God has put in the Church to rule the Church, watch out, for this is surely of the devil.
4. Forgets to praise partial progress (due to goal consciousness).
5. Can be misused if not properly judged (1 Corinthians 14:29).
6. Not all prophecies may be of God (2 Corinthians 11:3-4, 13-15; 2 Thessalonians 2:1-2).
7. The person giving the prophecy may be forbidden or hindered by leaders or the congregation (1 Thessalonians 5:19-20).

2. Gift of Helps/Service

Scriptures: Romans 12:6-8

Greek Usage: There are several Greek words in the Bible translated *help, service, ministry,* etc. The Greek word used in connection with the gifts or motives is the *diakonia*. The one in 1 Corinthians 12:28 is the *antilepsis*, which is mentioned nowhere else in the New Testament.

diakonos (SC1249) = "A servant of people, a waiter, attendant, servant or a minister." It is translated: *deacon, servant, minister.*

diakonia (SC1248) = "A service or ministry to the people. The service. Service or attendance as a servant." KJV translates this word: *ministry, ministering, serving, relief, office, service, administration.*

diakoneo (SC1247) = "To serve people, to be an attendant, to wait upon. The act of serving." KJV translates this word: *minister unto, serve, minister, administer, use of the office of a deacon, minister to.*

antilepsis (SC484) = Relief, from *antilambanomai*: "To take hold of in turn, i.e. succor; also to participate." It is translated: *help* (according to C.V. Bryant the word means "to aid and assist another in need," and the noun describes the acceptance between a person being helped and another person giving the help).

Various Definitions:

Bruce L. Bugbee: The Gift of Helps is the divine enablement to attach spiritual value to the accomplishment of physical tasks within the body of Christ. The Gift of Hospitality is the divine enablement to care for new or needy people by providing fellowship, food, or shelter.[58]

Kevin J. Conner: Those who help others, helpers, one who aids, assists or supports the weak, do others service.[59]

Frank Damazio: One who gives relief and help; one who lightens the load of leaders by doing certain practical things for them.[60]

Leslie B. Flynn: This carries the meaning of assistance, lending a hand.[61]

C. Peter Wagner: The gift of *helps* is the special ability that God gives to certain members of the body of Christ to invest the talents they have in the life and ministry of other members of the body, thus enabling the person helped to increase the effectiveness of his or her spiritual gifts. The gift of *service* is the special ability that God gives to certain members of the body of Christ to identify the unmet needs involved in a task related to God's work, and to make use of available resources to meet those needs and help accomplish the desired goals.[62]

Suggested Definition:

The supernatural Functional Gift that God gives to certain members of the body of Christ which enables them to invest their talents and available resources in the life and/or ministry of another in a manner that helps others accomplish their goals.

Good Biblical Example: Martha and Timothy

Various Characteristics and Potential Weaknesses:

Don and Katie Fortune[63]

Characteristics of the Server:

1. Easily recognizes practical needs and is quick to meet them.
2. Especially enjoys manual projects, jobs, and functions.
3. Keeps everything in meticulous order.
4. Is a detail person with a good memory.
5. Enjoys showing hospitality.
6. Will stay with something until it is completed.
7. Has a hard time saying no to requests for help.
8. Is more interested in meeting the needs of others than own needs.
9. Enjoys working on immediate goals rather than long-range goals.
10. Shows love for others in deeds and actions more than words.
11. Needs to feel appreciated.
12. Tends to do more than asked to do.
13. Feels greatest joy in doing something that is helpful.
14. Does not want to lead others or projects.
15. Has a high energy level.
16. Cannot stand to be around clutter.

17. Tends to be a perfectionist.
18. Views serving to be of primary importance in life.
19. Prefers doing a job to delegating it.
20. Supports others who are in leadership.

Problems of the Server:

1. Is critical of others who do not help out with obvious needs.
2. May neglect own family's needs by being too busy helping others.
3. May become pushy or interfering in eagerness to help.
4. Finds it hard to accept being served by others.
5. Is easily hurt when unappreciated.

Gothard[64]

Characteristics:

1. An ability to see *practical needs* and a desire to meet them.
2. A joy in serving when it *frees others* to do more important things, not just to keep busy.
3. A tendency to *disregard* personal *health* and *comfort* in serving others.
4. A *difficulty* in saying "no" resulting in a variety of involvements and a tendency to get sidetracked.
5. A special enjoyment in providing for *physical needs* and comforts. An ability to remember likes and dislikes.
6. A need for appreciation to confirm that service is necessary and satisfactory. A desire for clear instructions (without time limits).
7. A strong desire to be with others, thus providing more serving opportunities.
8. An enjoyment of short-range projects and a tendency to become frustrated with long-range responsibilities.
9. A tendency to feel inadequate and unqualified for spiritual leadership.

How Servers Can Misuse Their Gift:

1. Neglecting home responsibilities to help others.
2. Accepting too many jobs at one time.
3. Wearing themselves out physically.
4. Being too persistent in giving unrequested help to others.
5. Going around proper authorities in order to get jobs done.
6. Excluding others from helping on a job.
7. Interfering with God's discipline by premature help.
8. Becoming hurt by the ungratefulness of those who were helped.
9. Getting "sidetracked" while working on an assignment.

Hickey[65]

Characteristics:

1. Has ability to recall likes and dislikes of people.
2. Is alert to detect and meet practical needs.
3. Meets needs as quickly as possible.
4. Has physical stamina without regard of weariness.
5. Will use personal funds to avoid delay in meeting a need.
6. Needs to have sincere appreciation and can spot insincerity.
7. Wants to see a job done and will do extra work to accomplish it.
8. Is involved in a lot of activities because can't say "no."
9. Enjoys short-range goals more than long-range goals.
10. Is frustrated with time limits on jobs.

Misunderstandings:

1. When trying to meet needs may appear to be "pushy."
2. Will do jobs himself to avoid "red tape."
3. Eagerness to serve can be misconstrued as wanting to advance self.
4. May get upset with others when they don't have the same motive.
5. Finds it difficult to accept service from others.
6. Desire for appreciation may result in hurt feelings.
7. Desire to help others may interfere with God's dealings with others.

8. Meeting practical needs may be judged as lack of interest in spiritual needs.
9. Stamina may be misinterpreted as insensitivity to others desiring to serve, too.
10. Enjoyment with short-range goals may lead to frustration and disorganization with long-range goals.
11. May get sidetracked with other's needs instead of the pastor's directions.

Practical Christian Living Class Notes (pp. 39, 40)

Characteristics:

1. Sensitivity to see practical needs and a strong desire to meet them.
2. Deep joy in serving, especially when it releases others to get more involved in their ministry.
3. Tendency to overlook personal health and comfort in serving others.
4. Real difficulty in saying "no" and a tendency, therefore, to get sidetracked.
5. Keen memory and a special fulfillment in providing for the physical needs of others.
6. Need for appreciation to confirm that service is necessary and satisfactory.
7. Strong desire to be with others, thus providing greater opportunities for service.
8. Enjoyment of short-range goals; tendency to be frustrated with long-term projects.
9. Tendency to feel inadequate and unqualified for "spiritual" leadership.

In the Spirit	*In the Flesh*
Alert	Unaware
Hospitable	Lonely
Generous	Stingy
Joyful	Withdrawn (self-pity)
Flexible	Resistive
Available	Self-centered
Enduring	Quitter

Potential Problems:

1. May appear to be pushy.
2. May be judgmental toward others who do not see needs and meet them.
3. Sidesteps proper authorities to get job done fast.
4. Eagerness may appear to be self-seeking.
5. Has trouble delegating responsibility.
6. May neglect personal and family needs.
7. May interfere with "lessons" God is teaching those in need.
8. Is easily sidetracked.
9. Zeal to meet practical needs may be viewed as lack of interest in spiritual matters.
10. Personal stamina may be seen as insensitivity to others who are helping.
11. Is easily hurt when not appreciated.

***Suggested Characteristics*:**

1. Readily recognizes practical needs and is quick to meet those needs.
2. Feels a deep joy in serving, especially when it releases others to get more involved in their ministry (Romans 16:1-2).
3. Has a keen memory, remembering people's likes and dislikes.
4. Will stay with a project until it is completed. Perfectionist.
5. Is more interested in meeting needs of others than in own needs.
6. Enjoys working on projects with immediate goals instead of long-range goals; wants to see a job finished.
7. Would rather serve than lead others or projects.

***Suggested Potential Weaknesses*:**

1. May become pushy or interfering in own eagerness to help.
2. May neglect own family's needs by being too busy helping others.
3. May be critical of others who do not detect and meet obvious needs.
4. Finds it hard to accept being served by others.
5. Is easily hurt when unappreciated.
6. Can become overly occupied with much serving, even overlooking personal health.
7. Has real difficulty in saying "no."

3. Gift of Teaching

Scriptures: 1 Corinthians 12:28

Greek Usage: *didaskalia* (SC1321) and *didaskalos* (SC1320) Instruction, doctrine, learning, teaching. Occurs 21 times in the New Testament, of which 15 are found in the pastoral epistles.

Various Definitions:

Bruce L. Bugbee: The divine enablement to understand, clearly explain, and apply the Word of God to the lives of listeners.[66]

Kevin J. Conner: One who instructs, the occupation of teaching, someone qualified to instruct others, someone who imparts Bible truth to others.[67]

Frank Damazio: One who instructs others; one who instills doctrine into another.[68]

Leslie B. Flynn: More than impartation of information; it should lead to involvement of the individual.[69]

David Allen Hubbard: One who grasps the truths of Scripture and has unusual facility in explaining, illustrating, and applying them.[70]

C. Peter Wagner: The special ability that God gives to certain members of the body of Christ to communicate information relevant to the health and ministry of the body and its members in such a way that others will learn.[71]

Suggested Definition:

The supernatural Functional Gift that God gives to certain members of the body of Christ which enables them to communicate information relevant to the health and ministry of the body and its members in such a way that others will learn.

Good Biblical Example: Luke and Apollos

Various Characteristics and Potential Weaknesses:

Don and Katie Fortune[72]

Characteristics of the Teacher:

1. Presents truth in a logical, systematic way.
2. Validates truth by checking out the facts.
3. Loves to study and do research.
4. Enjoys word studies.
5. Prefers to use biblical illustrations rather than life illustrations.
6. Gets upset when Scripture is used out of context.
7. Feels concerned that truth be established in every situation.
8. Is more objective than subjective.
9. Easily develops and uses a large vocabulary.
10. Emphasizes facts and the accuracy of words.
11. Checks out the source of knowledge of others who teach.
12. Prefers teaching believers to engaging in evangelism.
13. Feels Bible study is foundational to the operation of all the gifts.
14. Solves problems by starting with scriptural principles.
15. Is intellectually sharp.
16. Is self-disciplined.
17. Is emotionally self-controlled.
18. Has only a select circle of friends.
19. Has strong convictions and opinions based on investigation of facts.
20. Believes truth has the intrinsic power to produce change.

Problems of the Teacher:

1. Tends to neglect the practical application of truth.
2. Is slow to accept viewpoints of others.
3. Tends to develop pride in intellectual ability.
4. Tends to be legalistic and dogmatic.
5. Is easily sidetracked by new interests.

Gothard[73]

Characteristics:

1. The need to validate truth; to certify statements which have been made by others.
2. The tendency to validate new truth by established systems of truth.
3. The prompting to give teaching credentials before speaking and to get them from others before listening.
4. The desire to present truth in a systematic sequence.
5. A delight in researching and reporting as many facts on a subject as possible.
6. An emphasis on the importance and accuracy of reporting.
7. An alertness to factual details which are not noticed or mentioned by others.
8. A tendency to remain silent until information has been heard, observed, and discussed.
9. A need to exercise diligence and endurance.

How Teachers Can Misuse Their Gift:

1. Becoming proud of their knowledge.
2. Despising the practical wisdom of uneducated people.
3. Communicating skepticism toward their teachers.
4. Criticizing sound teaching because of technical flaws.
5. Depending on human reasoning rather than the Holy Spirit's teaching.
6. Giving information which lacks practical application.
7. Boring listeners with details of research.
8. Retreating into their own world of books.

Marilyn Hickey[74]

Characteristics:

1. Belief that gift is foundational to other gifts.
2. Emphasis on accuracy of words.
3. Testing of knowledge of those who teach them.
4. Delight in research in order to validate truth.
5. Validating new information by established systems of truth.
6. Presenting truth in systematic sequence.
7. Avoidance of illustrations from non-Bible source.
8. Resistance to Scriptural illustrations out of context.
9. Greater joy in researching than in presenting lesson.

Misunderstandings:

1. Emphasis on accuracy of Scriptural interpretation may appear to neglect practical application.
2. Research of others may appear to be dependent on intellect instead of Holy Spirit.
3. Use of knowledge in testing others may appear to be pride of learning.
4. Details of research may appear to be unnecessary to listeners.
5. Objectivity in research may appear to lack warmth and feeling when speaking.

Practical Christian Living Class Notes (pp. 37, 38)

Characteristics:

1. Desire to present truth in a systematic sequence.
2. Emphasis on importance and accuracy of words.
3. Delight in researching and reporting as many facts as possible.
4. An alertness to factual details which are not noticed or mentioned by others.
5. A tendency to test the knowledge of those who are teaching. Need to validate truth.
6. Greater joy in researching truth than presenting it.

7. Tendency to avoid use of illustrations from non-biblical sources.
8. Tendency to remain silent until information has been heard and evaluated.
9. Tendency to validate new truth by established systems of truth.

In the Spirit	*In the Flesh*
Accurate	Careless
Reverent	Disrespectful
Diligent	Slothful
Thorough	Incomplete
Dependable	Inconsistent
Secure	Anxious
Patient	Restless

Potential Weaknesses:

1. Emphasizes accuracy at the expense of application. Lack of warmth.
2. Bores listeners with unnecessary details.
3. May appear to be more dependent on research of others than on the Holy Spirit.
4. Becomes proud of knowledge.
5. Lets teaching get ahead of living.
6. Concentrates on "pet" doctrines.
7. Gives impression that he or she is the only valid source of truth.
8. Criticizes teaching of others due to petty differences.
9. Discounts the wisdom of the uneducated.

Suggested Characteristics:

1. Presents truth in a logical, systematic way.
2. Loves to validate truth by intensive research.
3. Prefers teaching believers to engaging in evangelism.
4. Feels this gift is foundational to the operation of other gifts.
5. Earnestly desires to explain biblical principles to others.
6. Is concerned to help others learn what the Bible teaches about life.
7. Gets excited about acquiring knowledge out of God's Word.
8. Tends to draw illustrations and applications from biblical sources rather than non-biblical ones (Acts 17:2-3; 18:28).

Suggested Potential Weaknesses:

1. Emphasizes accuracy at the expense of application. Lacks warmth.
2. Bores listeners with unnecessary details.
3. May appear to be more dependent on research of others than on the Holy Spirit.
4. Becomes proud of knowledge.
5. Lets teaching get ahead of living.
6. Concentrates on "pet" doctrines.
7. Gives impression that he or she is the only valid source of truth.
8. Criticizes teaching of others due to petty differences.
9. Discounts the wisdom of the uneducated.

4. Gift of Exhortation/Encouragement

Scriptures: Romans 12:6-8

Greek Usage: *parakleesis* (SC3874) from *parakaleo* (SC3870) To comfort, console, exhort, entreat.

Various Definitions:

Bruce L. Bugbee: The divine enablement to reassure, strengthen, and affirm those who are discouraged or wavering in their faith.[75]

Kevin J. Conner: To warn, to admonish, to be cheered or comforted, to entreat, to urge, persuasion or excitement.[76]

Frank Damazio: One who consoles, encourages, strengthens others; one who comforts others on a personal level; one who encourages the Church with short words of edification.[77]

Leslie B. Flynn: The gift of exhortation involves the supernatural ability to come alongside to help, to strengthen the weak, reassure the wavering, console the troubled, encourage the halting.[78]

C. Peter Wagner: The special ability that God gives to certain members of the body of Christ to minister words of comfort, consolation, encouragement, and counsel to other members of the body of Christ in such a way that they feel helped and healed.[79]

Suggested Definition:

The supernatural Functional Gift that God gives to certain members of the body of Christ to encourage, stimulate faith and counsel, and support and strengthen those in the body of Christ in such a way that they feel helped and healed.

Good Biblical Example: Paul and Barnabas

Various Characteristics and Potential Weaknesses:

Don and Katie Fortune[80]

Characteristics:

1. Loves to encourage others to live victoriously.
2. Wants a visible response when teaching or speaking.
3. Prefers to apply truth rather than research it.
4. Prefers systems of information that have practical application.
5. Loves to prescribe precise steps of action to aid personal growth.
6. Focuses on working with people.
7. Encourages others to develop in their personal ministries.
8. Finds truth in experience and then validates it with Scripture.
9. Loves to do personal counseling.
10. Will discontinue personal counseling if no effort to change is seen.
11. Is fluent in communication.
12. Views trials as opportunities to produce personal growth.
13. Accepts people as they are without judging them.
14. Is greatly loved because of his positive attitude.
15. Prefers witnessing with life rather than verbal witnessing.
16. Makes decisions easily.
17. Usually completes what is started.
18. Wants to clear up problems with others quickly.
19. Expects a lot of self and others.
20. Needs a "sounding board" for bouncing off ideas and thoughts.

Problems of the Exhorter:

1. Tends to interrupt others in eagerness to give opinions or advice.
2. Will use Scriptures out of context in order to make a point.
3. May be "cut and dried" in prescribing steps of action.
4. Is outspokenly opinionated.
5. Can become overly self-confident.

Gothard[81]

Characteristics:

1. A motivation to urge people to their *full spiritual maturity* in Christ.
2. An ability to discern *where a person is* in spiritual growth and to speak on that level.
3. A desire to give *precise steps* of action in urging people toward spiritual maturity.
4. A drive to explain truth with *logical reasoning* in order to make it accepted.
5. An ability to *visualize spiritual achievement* for people and to use this to motivate them to action.
6. A desire for face to face discussion in order to determine and insure a positive response.
7. An ability to identify with people of different types and backgrounds in order to gain a wider hearing.
8. A motivation to bring harmony between diverse groups of Christians, and an awareness that harmony is basic to spiritual maturity.
9. An ability to welcome personal tribulation as a chief motivator of spiritual growth.

How Exhorters Can Misuse Their Gift:

1. Raising the expectations of others prematurely.
2. Taking "family time" to counsel others.
3. Treating family and friends as "projects" rather than persons.
4. Sharing private illustrations without permission.
5. Jumping into new projects without finishing existing ones.
6. Encouraging others to depend on them rather than God and their authorities.
7. Trusting visible results rather than a true change of heart.
8. Neglecting proper emphasis on basic Bible doctrines.
9. Giving counsel before discerning the type of person or problem.

Hickey[82]

Characteristics:

1. Desire to visualize specific achievement and give steps of action.
2. Tendency to avoid systems of information that lack practical application.
3. Ability to see how tribulation can produce new levels of maturity.
4. Dependence on individual acceptance when speaking to people.
5. Insights in human experience that can be applied to the Bible.
6. Enjoyment in seeing people take steps of action to meet needs.
7. Grief when teaching doesn't have practical application.
8. Delight in personal conferences that result in new insights.

Misunderstandings:

1. Emphasis on steps of action may seem to oversimplify the problem.
2. Urgency in giving steps of action may appear as having more confidence in them.
3. Desire to win non-Christians by living examples may appear as lack of interest in personal evangelism.
4. Use of Scripture for practical application may appear to take it out of context.
5. Emphasis in steps of action may appear not to have awareness of others' feelings.

Practical Christian Living Class Notes (pp. 29, 30)

Characteristics:

1. Strong desire to urge people on to their full spiritual maturity.
2. Ability to visualize spiritual goals of people and to use this to motivate them to action.
3. Ability to discern where people are in their spiritual growth and to speak to that level of maturity.
4. Motivation to give specific steps of action in encouraging people on in their spiritual growth.

5. Openness to personal suffering as a means to motivate spiritual growth.
6. Deep satisfaction with those eager to grow spiritually.
7. Tendency to reject sources of information that lack personal application.
8. Desire for face-to-face encounters in order to promote a positive response.
9. Look for human experience which can be supported in Scripture.
10. Motivation to promote harmony between diverse groups of Christians.
11. Ability to identify with all kinds of people in order to gain a wider hearing.

In the Spirit	*In the Flesh*
Discernment	Judgment
Wisdom	Natural Inclination
Faith	Presumption
Discretion	Simple-mindedness
Self-control	Self-gratification
Creativity	Underachievement
Enthusiasm	Apathy

Potential Weaknesses:

1. Emphasis on steps to solution may appear to over-simplify the problem.
2. Taking Scripture out of context for the sake of practical application.
3. Subtle insensitivity to sin.
4. Tendency to neglect own circle of relationships in order to minister to others.
5. Emphasis on importance of "living the life" may appear as a lack of interest in soul winning.

6. Spending too much time with an individual.
7. Inadvertently causing dependency on exhorter rather than God and self.
8. Reliance on outward change rather than change of heart.
9. Inability to be exhorted.

Suggested Characteristics:

1. Loves to prescribe precise steps of action to aid personal growth (Romans 12:1-2).
2. Enjoys working with those eager to follow steps of action (Proverbs 13:10).
3. Will encourage others to develop in their personal ministry (Philippians 3:17).
4. Finds truth in experience and validates it with Scripture (James 1:22).
5. Loves to do personal counseling (1 Timothy 4:11-16).
6. Dislikes teaching that is not followed by practical application (James 2:18).
7. Accepts people where they are. Non-judgmental (1 Corinthians 4:4-5).
8. Loves to encourage others to live victoriously (Philippians 4:6; Acts 11:23).
9. Usually completes what is started (2 Timothy 4:7).
10. Expects a lot of self and others (Ephesians 4:1; Galatians 6:9).

Suggested Potential Weaknesses:

1. Tends to interrupt others in eagerness to give advice or opinion.
2. Prefers to witness with the life rather than through verbal witnessing.
3. Will use Scriptures out of context in order to make a point.
4. May be "cut-and-dried" in prescribing steps of action to conceal.
5. Emphasis on steps of action may appear to oversimplify the problem.
6. Can become overly confident in prescribed steps of action.

5. Gift of Giving

Scriptures: Romans 12:6-8

Greek Usage: *metadidomi* (SC3330) To give, share, impart.

Various Definitions:

Bruce L. Bugbee: The divine enablement and ability to contribute money and material resources to the work of the Lord with cheerfulness and liberality.[83]

Kevin J. Conner: He that imparts, to share, to bestow, a distributor of alms, to give a part of what we have.[84]

Frank Damazio: One who liberally shares and imparts to others what he has to give; one who gives to others out of the abundance that God has given to him.[85]

Leslie B. Flynn: The gift of giving involves giving simply, with singleness of mind, mental honesty — without pretense. When one gives from an openness of heart, one donates freely with delight. Moreover, he gives generously, with liberality.[86]

C. Peter Wagner: The special ability that God gives to certain members of the body of Christ to contribute their material resources to the work of the Lord with liberality and cheerfulness.[87]

Suggested Definition:

The supernatural Functional Gift that God gives to certain members of the body of Christ to contribute their material resources to the work of the Lord with liberality and cheerfulness.

Good Biblical Example: Matthew and Abraham

Various Characteristics and Potential Weaknesses:

Don and Katie Fortune[88]

Characteristics of the Giver:

1. Gives freely of money, possessions, time, energy, and love.
2. Loves to give without others knowing about it.
3. Wants to feel a part of the ministries to which he contributes.
4. Intercedes for needs and the salvation of souls.
5. Feels delighted when his gift is an answer to specific prayer.
6. Wants gifts to be of high quality or craftsmanship.
7. Gives only by the leading of the Holy Spirit.
8. Gives to support and bless others or to advance a ministry.
9. Views hospitality as an opportunity to give.
10. Handles finances with wisdom and frugality.
11. Quickly volunteers to help where a need is seen.
12. Seeks confirmation on the amount to give.
13. Has a strong belief in tithing and in giving in addition to tithing.
14. Focuses on sharing the Gospel.
15. Believes God is the Source of his supply.
16. Is very industrious with a tendency toward success.
17. Has natural and effective business ability.
18. Likes to get the best value for the money spent.
19. Is definitely not gullible.
20. Possesses both natural and God-given wisdom.

Problems of the Giver:

1. May try to control how contributions are used.
2. Tends to pressure others to give.
3. May upset family and friends with unpredictable patterns of giving.
4. Tends to spoil own children or other relatives.
5. May use financial giving to get out of responsibilities.

Gothard[89]

Characteristics:

1. A keen ability to discern *wise investments* in order to have more money available to give away.
2. A desire to *give quietly* without public notice.
3. A motivation to give as unto the Lord at His promptings, not at man's appeals.
4. A desire to give gifts which are of *high quality.*
5. An ability to *test faithfulness* and wisdom by how people handle funds.
6. A tendency to practice personal frugality. An ability to be content with the basic necessities of life.
7. An alertness to see what other people do with their money.
8. An ability to see financial needs which others tend to overlook.
9. A desire to use giving as a way to motivate others to give.

How Givers Can Misuse Their Gift:

1. Giving too sparingly to their own family.
2. Causing a family to resent gifts to others.
3. Listening to unscriptural counsel on money management.
4. Putting pressure on people who have less to give.
5. Failing to discern God's promptings for a gift.
6. Judging those who misuse funds rather than advising them.
7. Controlling people or ministries by gifts.
8. Corrupting people by giving too much.
9. Investing in projects which do not benefit the lives of people.

Hickey[90]

Characteristics:

1. Ability to make wise purchases and investments.
2. Desire to give quietly to effective ministries and projects.
3. Attempt to use his giving to motivate others to give.

4. Alertness to valid needs he fears others may overlook.
5. Enjoyment in meeting needs without pressure of appeals.
6. Joy when his gift is an answer to another's prayer.
7. Dependency on partner's counsel to confirm amount of gift.
8. Concern that his gift be of high quality.
9. Desire to feel a part of the work or person to whom he gives.

Misunderstandings:

1. Need to deal with large sums of money may appear to focus on temporal values.
2. Desire to give to a ministry may appear as an attempt to control the work or person.
3. Attempt to encourage others to give may appear as lack of generosity and unnecessary pressure.
4. Lack of response to pressure appeals may appear to be lack of generosity.
5. Living personally frugal may appear to others as selfishness in not meeting friends' or relatives' needs.

Practical Christian Living Class Notes (pp. 31, 32)

Characteristics:

1. Ability to make wise investments and purchases in order to have more to give away.
2. A desire to give quietly without public fanfare.
3. Motivation to give according to God's leading, not man's appeals.
4. A desire to give as a means of motivating others to give.
5. Keen sensitivity to the financial needs which others may overlook.
6. Ability to test faithfulness and wisdom by way others handle money.
7. Practice of personal frugality; content with basic necessities.
8. Experience of great joy when giving is an answer to prayer.
9. Desire to give gifts of high quality.
10. A desire to feel a part of the person or work to whom he gives.

In the Spirit	*In the Flesh*
Thrifty	Extravagant
Resourceful	Wasteful
Content	Covetous
Punctual	Tardy
Tolerant	Prejudiced
Cautious	Impulsive
Grateful	Ungrateful

Potential Weaknesses:

1. May appear to be materialistically-minded because of emphasis on money and things.
2. Lack of interest in pressure appeals may appear as lack of generosity.
3. Attempt to interest others in giving may be interpreted as inappropriate.
4. May get ahead of God in their giving.
5. Appear to be more interested in projects than people.
6. May be so frugal as to cause resentment among family members.
7. Their giving may seem foolish to those who do not have the gift.
8. Desire to increase effectiveness of ministry may appear as an attempt to control group or person.

Suggested Characteristics:

1. Ability to make wise purchases and investments in order to set aside more resources for the Lord (Matthew 25:14-23).
2. Desire to give quietly to effective ministries and projects (Matthew 6:4).
3. Attempt to use his giving to motivate others to give (Luke 6:38).
4. Alertness to valid needs he fears others may overlook (Proverbs 19:7; 22:9).
5. Enjoyment in meeting needs without pressure of appeals (Matthew 10:8).
6. Joy when his gift is an answer to another's prayer (2 Corinthians 9:7).
7. Concern that his gift be of high quality (Matthew 2:11; Luke 7:37, 38).
8. Desire to feel a part of the work or person to whom he gives (Luke 8:1-3; Acts 4:37).
9. Readiness to give regularly (2 Corinthians 8:7; 1 Corinthians 16:2).

Suggested Potential Weaknesses:

1. Need to deal with large sums of money may appear to focus on temporal values.
2. Desire to give to a ministry may appear as attempt to control the work or person.
3. Attempt to encourage others to give may appear as lack of generosity and unnecessary pressure.
4. Lack of response to pressure appeals may appear to be lack of generosity.
5. Living personally frugal may appear to others as selfishness in not meeting friends' or relatives' needs.
6. Giving out of hope of big gain might cross line of trusting God to forcing Him.
7. The desire to abuse this gift to get from the saints.

6. Gift of Administration/Government/Leadership

Scriptures: Administration — 1 Corinthians 12:28; Leadership — Romans 12:6-8

Greek Usage: *kubernesis* (SC2941) Administration/Government — To steer, pilotage, directorship, government

proisteemi (SC4291) Leadership — To stand before, to preside, maintain, be over, rule.

Various Definitions:

Bruce L. Bugbee: The Gift of Administration is the divine enablement to understand what makes an organization function, and the special ability to plan, execute, and achieve procedures that increase the church's organizational effectiveness. The Gift of Leadership is the divine enablement to attract, lead, and motivate people to accomplish the work of ministry.[91]

Kevin J. Conner: He that takes the lead, to set before, appoint with authority, to preside, govern, superintend.[92]

Frank Damazio: One who presides over various Church functions; one who leads by good example and service; one who organizes, facilitates and administrates church activities; one who steers, directs or pilots an activity in the Church or local church.[93]

Leslie B. Flynn: The Spirit-given ability to preside, govern, plan, organize, and administer with wisdom, fairness, example, humility, service, confidence, ease and efficiency.[94]

B. E. Underwood: The ability to organize and direct the activities of the church so that she will fulfill her mission.[95]

C. Peter Wagner: The special ability that God gives to certain members of the body of Christ to understand clearly the immediate and long-range goals of a particular unit of the body of Christ and to devise effective plans for the accomplishment of those goals.[96]

Suggested Definition:

The supernatural Functional Gift that God gives to certain members of the body of Christ to plan, organize, and direct the activities to implement His will.

Good Biblical Example: Joseph and Nehemiah

Various Characteristics and Potential Weaknesses:

***Don and Katie Fortune*[97]**

Characteristics of the Administrator:

1. Is highly motivated to organize that for which he's responsible.
2. Expresses ideas and organization in ways that communicate clearly.
3. Prefers to be under authority in order to have authority.
4. Will not take responsibility unless delegated by those in authority.
5. Will assume responsibilities if no specific leadership exists.
6. Especially enjoys working on long-range goals and projects.
7. Is a visionary person with a broad perspective.
8. Easily facilitates resources and people to accomplish tasks or goals.
9. Enjoys delegating tasks and supervising people.
10. Will endure criticism in order to accomplish the ultimate task.
11. Has great zeal and enthusiasm for whatever he is involved in.
12. Finds greatest fulfillment and joy in working to accomplish goals.
13. Is willing to let others get the credit in order to get a job done.
14. Prefers to move on to a new challenge once something is completed.
15. Constantly writes notes to self.
16. Is a natural and capable leader.
17. Knows when to keep old methods going and when to introduce new ones.
18. Enjoys working with and being around people.
19. Wants to see things completed as quickly as possible.
20. Does not enjoy doing routine tasks.

Problems of the Administrator:

1. Becomes upset when others do not share the same vision or goals.
2. Develops outer callousness due to being a target for criticism.
3. Can regress into "using" people to accomplish own goals.

4. Tends to drive self and neglect personal and family needs.
5. Neglects routine home responsibilities due to intense interest in "job."

Gothard[98]

Characteristics:

1. An ability to *visualize* the *final result* of a major undertaking.
2. An ability to break down major goals into smaller, achievable tasks.
3. An ability to know what *resources are available and needed* to reach a goal.
4. A tendency to remove himself from *distracting details* in order to focus on the ultimate goal.
5. A willingness to *endure reaction* from insiders and outsiders in order to reach an ultimate goal.
6. A need for loyalty and confidence from those who are being directed and served.
7. An ability to know what he should and should not delegate to others.
8. An ability to inspire and encourage workers by cheerfulness, approval, praise, and challenges.
9. A joy and fulfillment in seeing all the parts come together in a finished product.

How Administrators Can Misuse Their Gift:

1. Viewing people as "human resources" rather than human beings.
2. Using people to accomplish personal ambitions.
3. Showing favoritism to those who appear to be more loyal.
4. Taking charge of projects which were not God's direction.
5. Delegating too much work to others.
6. Overlooking serious character faults in valuable workers.
7. Being unresponsive to suggestions and appeals.
8. Failing to give proper explanations and praise to workers.

Hickey[99]

Characteristics:

1. Ability to see overall picture and clarify long-range goals.
2. Motivation to organize what he is responsible for.
3. Desire to complete tasks as quickly as possible.
4. Awareness of resources available to complete a task.
5. Ability to know what can and cannot be delegated.
6. Tendency to stand on sidelines until those in charge tell him to take over.
7. Tendency to assume responsibility if no structured leadership exists.
8. Willingness to endure reactions from workers in order to accomplish ultimate tasks.
9. Fulfillment in seeing others coming together and enjoying a completed task.
10. Desire to move on to a new challenge when a previous task is completed.

Misunderstandings:

1. The ability to delegate responsibilities may appear to be laziness.
2. Willingness to endure reaction may appear as callousness.
3. Neglect in explaining why tasks must be done may prompt workers to think they are being misused.
4. Viewing people as resources may appear that projects are more important than people.
5. The desire to complete tasks swiftly may appear to be insensitive to the schedules, weariness, or priorities of workers.

Practical Christian Living Class Notes (pp. 33, 34)

Characteristics:

1. The ability to see the overall picture and to visualize the final result of a major project.
2. A self-starter; able to take charge immediately.
3. An ability to know what resources are required and available to reach a goal.
4. An ability to know what to delegate to others.
5. A tendency to stay removed from details in order to keep focused on the ultimate goal.
6. Extreme loyalty, requiring the same from those who are being led.
7. A desire to complete tasks as quickly as possible.
8. Great joy in seeing the job completed.
9. Ability to inspire and encourage workers by cheerfulness, approval, praise, and challenges.
10. A desire to move on to a new challenge when a previous project is completed.

In the Spirit	*In the Flesh*
Orderly	Disorganized
Showing initiative	Unresponsive
Responsible	Irresponsible
Humble	Proud
Decisive	Double-minded
Determined	Faint-hearted
Loyal	Unfaithful

Potential Weaknesses:

1. Ability to delegate may appear as laziness or avoiding work.
2. Desire to meet goals quickly may give appearance of a "slave driver."
3. Ability to handle "flak" well may give appearance of callousness.
4. Viewing people as resources may be seen as considering projects to be more important than people.
5. Tendency to disregard people with character flaws who are needed to accomplish goals.
6. Failure to explain adequately why work must be done may cause others to conclude they are being used.
7. Equating of leadership with greatness.
8. Equating of leadership with dynamic personality.
9. Failure to exercise gift fully for fear of failing.

Suggested Characteristics:

1. Ability to see overall picture and clarify long-range goals (Nehemiah 1:2-3; 2:5).
2. Motivation to organize what he is responsible for.
3. Desire to complete tasks as quickly as possible.
4. Awareness of resources available to complete a task.
5. Ability to know what can and cannot be delegated (Nehemiah 4:13).
6. Tendency to stand on sidelines until those in charge tell him to take over.
7. Tendency to assume responsibility if no structured leadership exists.
8. Willingness to endure reactions from workers in order to accomplish ultimate tasks (Nehemiah 4:4-18).
9. Fulfillment in seeing others coming together and enjoying a completed task (Nehemiah 7:1-2; 8:1-18).
10. Desire to move on to a new challenge when a previous task is completed.
11. Willingness to be accountable to the whole body, seeking and executing its guidelines.

Suggested Potential Weaknesses:

1. Delegating responsibilities may appear as laziness.
2. Willingness to endure reaction may appear as callousness.
3. Neglect in explaining why tasks must be done may prompt workers to think they are being misused.
4. Viewing people as resources may make it appear that projects are more important than people.
5. The desire to complete tasks swiftly may appear to be insensitivity to the schedules, weariness, and priorities of workers.

7. Gift of Showing Mercy

Scriptures: Romans 12:6-8

Greek Usage: *eleeo* (SC1653) To have pity, be compassionate, extend help for the consequence of sin.

Various Definitions:

Bruce L. Bugbee: The divine enablement to minister cheerfully and appropriately to people who are suffering.[100]

Kevin J. Conner: Have compassion, to show gracious favour, saving mercy towards.[101]

Frank Damazio: One who feels the hurts of others; one who is loving and compassionate; one who shows sincere, gracious favor to others; one who is motivated to encourage and cheer.[102]

Leslie B. Flynn: Help directed toward the saint in distress, the outcast, the poor, the underprivileged, the ill, the deprived, the handicapped, the retarded, the unlovely, the shut-in, the hungry, the alcoholic.[103]

C. Peter Wagner: The special ability that God gives to certain members of the body of Christ to feel genuine empathy and compassion for individuals, both Christian and non-Christian, who suffer distressing physical, mental, or emotional problems, and to translate that compassion into cheerfully-done deeds that reflect Christ's love and alleviate the suffering.[104]

Suggested Definition:

The supernatural Functional Gift that God gives to certain members of the body of Christ to respond wholeheartedly with extraordinary compassion to those who are in need, particularly spiritually.

Good Biblical Example: John the Beloved and the Good Samaritan

Various Characteristics and Potential Weaknesses:

Don and Katie Fortune[105]

Characteristics of the Compassion Person:

1. Has tremendous capacity to show love.
2. Always looks for good in people.
3. Senses the spiritual and emotional atmosphere of a group or individual.
4. Is attracted to people who are hurting or in distress.
5. Takes action to remove hurts and relieve distress in others.
6. Is more concerned for mental and emotional distress than physical distress.
7. Is motivated to help people have right relationships with one another.
8. Loves opportunities to give preference or place to others.
9. Takes care with words and actions to avoid hurting others.
10. Easily detects insincerity or wrong motives.
11. Is drawn to others with the gift of compassion.
12. Loves to do thoughtful things for others.
13. Is trusting and trustworthy.
14. Avoids conflicts and confrontations.
15. Doesn't like to be rushed in a job or activity.
16. Is typically cheerful and joyful.
17. Is ruled by the heart rather than the head.
18. Rejoices to see others blessed and grieves to see others hurt.
19. Is a crusader for good causes.
20. Intercedes for the hurts and problems of others.

Problems of the Compassion Person:

1. Tends to be indecisive.
2. Is often prone to take up another person's offense.
3. Is easily hurt by others.
4. Empathizes too much with the suffering of others.
5. Affectionate nature is often misinterpreted by opposite sex.

Gothard[106]

Characteristics:

1. An ability to sense *genuine love*. A greater vulnerability to deeper and more frequent hurts from the lack of love.
2. A need for *deep friendships* in which there is mutual commitment.
3. A tendency to react *harshly* when intimate friends are rejected.
4. A greater concern over *mental joy or distress* than physical concerns.
5. A tendency to *attract* people who are having mental and emotional distress.
6. A need to measure acceptance by physical closeness and quality time together.
7. A desire to remove the cause of hurts rather than to look for benefits from them.
8. A tendency to avoid decisions and firmness unless they will eliminate greater hurts.
9. A tendency to be attracted to those with the spiritual gift of prophecy.

How Those Gifted With Mercy Can Misuse Their Gift:

1. Failing to be firm and decisive when necessary.
2. Taking up offenses for those who have been hurt.
3. Basing decisions on emotions rather than on reason.
4. Promoting improper affections from those of the opposite sex.
5. Cutting off fellowship with those who are insensitive to others.
6. Reacting to God's purposes in allowing people to suffer.
7. Sympathizing with those who are violating God's standards.
8. Establishing possessive friendships with others.

Hickey[107]

Characteristics:

1. Ability to feel atmosphere of joy or distress in individual or group.
2. Attraction to and understanding of people in distress.
3. Desire to remove hurts from other's lives.
4. Greater concern for mental distress than physical distress.
5. Avoidance of being firm unless can see how brings benefits.
6. Sensitivity to words and actions that can hurt others.
7. Ability to discern true motives of people.
8. Enjoying of unity with others who are sensitive to people's needs.
9. Closing of spirit to those insincere or insensitive.

Misunderstandings:

1. Avoidance of firmness may appear to be weakness.
2. Sensitivity to spirit and feelings may cause others to believe they are led by emotions and not reason.
3. Attraction to those upset may be misinterpreted as interest in opposite sex.
4. Sensitivity to words and actions that cause hurt may be misinterpreted as taking up another's offense.
5. Ability to detect insincere motives may cause person to be hard to get to know.

Practical Christian Living Class Notes (pp. 35, 36)

Characteristics:

1. Ability to sense joy or pain in an individual or a group.
2. An attraction to and an understanding for people who are in distress.
3. A greater concern for mental anguish than physical distress.
4. A desire to remove the cause of hurts rather than look for the benefit of them.
5. Tendency to avoid firmness unless it will eliminate more hurts.
6. A sensitivity to words and actions which will hurt other people.

7. Tendency to react harshly when close friends are rejected.
8. An ability to sense genuine love. (Extremely vulnerable to deep hurt due to the lack of love.)
9. A need for deep friendships in which there is mutual commitment.
10. Great need for physical closeness and quality time with loved ones.
11. Ability to sense insincerity in others, and be closed to them.
12. Tendency to be attracted to and repelled by those with the gift of prophecy.

In the Spirit	*In the Flesh*
Attentive	Unconcerned
Sensitive	Callous
Fair	Partial
Compassionate	Indifferent
Gentle	Harsh
Showing deference	Rude
Meek	Angry

Potential Weaknesses:

1. Avoidance of firmness may be viewed as weakness.
2. Tends to be guided by emotions rather than reason and logic.
3. May view pain and suffering in an unscriptural manner.
4. Empathy with the hurts of others may evoke the wrong response in the opposite sex.
5. May be judgmental toward those with less "sensitive" gifts, such as prophecy, teaching, and exhortation.
6. May over-sympathize with those who are suffering because of sin in their lives.
7. The ability to detect insincere motives may cause others to feel a person with the gift of mercy is cold, distant, and hard to get to know.

Suggested Characteristics:

1. Easily discerns the motives of people (1 John 4:1-3).
2. Looks for the good in people. Is non-critical (Jude 23).
3. Senses the spiritual and emotional atmosphere of a group (Philemon 7).
4. Is attracted to people who are hurting or in distress (1 John 3:17, 18).
5. Wants to remove hurts and relieve distress (1 John 3:19-20).
6. Is motivated to help people to have right relationships with one another (1 John 2:9-11).
7. Loves opportunities to give place to others (Romans 12:8).
8. Takes care with words and actions to avoid hurting others (1 John 2:1).
9. Easily detects insincerity in others (1 John 2:4).
10. Is drawn to others with the gift of compassion.
11. Is thoughtful. Loves to do things for others. Remembers special occasions (1 John 3:18).
12. Trusts. Expects others to be honest and reliable (3 John 5, 6).
13. Lacks firmness unless it's seen how it will bring benefit (3 John 9-11).

Suggested Potential Weaknesses:

1. Tends to be indecisive.
2. Tends to be guided by emotions more than logic.
3. The tenderness and sensitivity can cause them to take up another person's offense.
4. Can be easily hurt by others.
5. Can let the empathy for the suffering of others infiltrate own mind or body.
6. Must be very careful in ministering to opposite sex. Compassion can be misinterpreted.
7. May exhibit pity when the person in need requires exhortation or reproof and therefore may hinder healing or growth.
8. May concentrate more on the physical needs than on helping the people spiritually.
9. May concentrate more on soul-winning and ignore the physical needs.

The Gifts of the Holy Spirit — The Manifestation Gifts

The following material deals with the gifts that have been listed in the third column, "Most Recognized Classification" — The Gifts of the Holy Spirit. Each gift has been listed separately, along with the corresponding scriptural references. Also given is the Greek usage for each gift. The corresponding number from Strong's Concordance is noted to help those who are not Greek scholars (e.g., SC4396).

We then have quoted definitions from scholars from various persuasions who have written on the subject, followed by our suggested definition. Finally, we have listed strengths and weaknesses of these gifts.

MOST RECOGNIZED CLASSIFICATION

Gifts of Christ	Functional Gifts	Gifts of the Holy Spirit	Gifts Prioritized By God	Gifts of God
Equipping Gifts	**Motivational Gifts**	**(Spiritual Charismata)**	**God-Appointed**	**(all talents)**
Ascension Gifts		**Manifestation Gifts**		
5-Fold Ministry Gifts				
Ministry Gifts				
Domata	*Charismata*	*Charismata*		
Ephesians 4:11-12	Romans 12:6-8	1 Corinthians 12:8-10	1 Corinthians 12:27-30	James 1:17
Apostles	Prophecy	Word of Wisdom	Apostles	
Prophets	Serving	Word of Knowledge	Prophets	
Evangelists	Teaching	Faith	Teachers	
Pastors	Exhorting	Gifts of Healing	Miracles	
Teachers	Giving	Working of Miracles	Gifts of Healing	
	Leading	Prophecy	Helps	
	Showing Mercy	Distinguishing of Spirits	Administration	
		Kinds of Tongues	Kinds of Tongues	
		Interpretation of Tongues	Interpretation of Tongues	

1. Word of Wisdom

Scriptures: 1 Corinthians 12:8

Greek Usage: *sophia* (SC4678) Wisdom.

Various Definitions:

Bruce L. Bugbee: The divine enablement to apply knowledge effectively.[108]

Kevin J. Conner: The quality of being wise by the Holy Spirit, a flash revelation given by the Spirit.[109]

Frank Damazio: One who receives supernatural revelation and wisdom from God for situations; one who is anointed by the Spirit to give specific counsel to others that meets their needs.[110]

Leslie B. Flynn: The ability to apply knowledge to vexing situations, to weigh their true nature, to exercise spiritual insight into rightness or wrongness of a complex state of affairs.[111]

R. M. Riggs: Imparted to those who preach as they present convincing arguments in the power of the Spirit; the ability and disposition to use infinite knowledge in the most profitable way, i.e. advice, guidance, government and personal revelation.[112]

C. Peter Wagner: The special ability that God gives to certain members of the body of Christ to know the mind of the Holy Spirit in such a way as to receive insight into how given knowledge may best be applied to specific needs arising in the body of Christ.[113]

J. Rodman Williams: A Word of wisdom is in some way an explication of the mystery of God that centers in Jesus Christ. Paul also speaks of Christ Himself as our wisdom: "...Christ Jesus, whom God made our wisdom" (1 Corinthians 1:30). Accordingly, that which speaks of Christ, particularly the wonder of the cross, is an utterance or word of wisdom. Such a word is spoken out of the mystery of God and glorifies Jesus Christ.... Though the primary and authoritative revelation of God's mystery was given to the Apostle Paul, other believers through the Holy Spirit may likewise receive revelation (cf. 1 Corinthians 14:26) and out of such revelation declare the truth of God. Such an utterance, accordingly is a word of wisdom.[114]

Suggested Definition:

The supernatural Manifestation Gift that God gives to members of the body of Christ that enables them to receive instant insight on how a situation, a scripture, a teaching, a revelation (word of knowledge, prophecy) may best be applied to a specific situation or need arising in the body of Christ, or how a given situation or need is to be resolved or helped or healed.

Suggested Characteristics:

1. Is a practical problem solver (Genesis 41:35-37; 1 Kings 3:16-28; Acts 16:1-4).
2. Receives understanding from the Lord about the best way to handle a situation or problem (Acts 15:28).
3. Often senses an awareness of how to pray or otherwise act to particular needs (Acts 16:25-31).

Suggested Potential Weaknesses:

1. May tend to appear to be authoritative in telling others how to act.
2. Tends to make decisions too quickly.
3. Can become proud.
4. Can use gift to manipulate people or unwittingly cause others to be dependent upon the one with the gift.
5. Could cause problems if gift is not shared in love.

2. Word of Knowledge

Scriptures: 1 Corinthians 12:8

Greek Usage: *gnosis* (sc1108) Meaning *knowing* or *the act of knowing*. Has a variety of applications with many implications, for example, *to allow, be aware of, feel, have knowledge, perceive, understand.*

Various Definitions:

Bruce L. Bugbee: The divine enablement to accumulate and analyze information effectively.[115]

Kevin Conner: The fact or state of knowing by the Holy Spirit. A revelation of facts not known by natural understanding as given by the Spirit.[116]

Frank Damazio: One who receives from God supernatural facts and information which would be humanly impossible to know.[117]

Leslie B. Flynn: The gift that enables the believer to search, systematize, and summarize the teaching of the Word of God.[118]

R. M. Riggs: Revelation of divine truth by the Spirit of truth; a revelation of facts and happenings; a giving of the word of knowledge.[119]

C. Peter Wagner: The special ability that God gives to certain members of the body of Christ to discover, accumulate, analyze, and clarify information and ideas that are pertinent to the growth and well-being of the Body.[120]

J. Rodman Williams: A Word of Knowledge is speaking of inspired knowledge, an articulation of truth that in its very utterance edifies the gathered body of believers . . . The Holy Spirit enables the one who so speaks to declare truth in a way totally beyond his own natural capacity or experience . . . The words, while being framed by the mind of the speaker, spring from a higher source . . . Accordingly they are oracular utterances . . . as used in teaching.[121]

Suggested Definition:

The supernatural Manifestation Gift that God gives to certain members of the body of Christ which consists of a revelation of facts about a person or situation, which is not learned through the efforts of the natural mind, but is a fragment of knowledge freely given by God, disclosing the truth which the Spirit wishes to be made known concerning a particular person or situation.

Suggested Characteristics:

1. Is able to speak forth by divine revelation the specific facts about a situation (Matthew 21:2; Mark 14:13-15; Acts 5:1-3).
2. Is able to reveal to individuals or groups their specific needs (John 4:16-26; Acts 9:11-12, 17; Luke 5:2-4).
3. Receives supernatural facts or information (Matthew 16:16-17; Acts 10:19).
4. Is able to discern the voice of the Lord (Acts 10:17-23).
5. Shows humility and childlikeness (Luke 10:21).
6. Is able to discern what is in a man's heart (Acts 14:9; John 2:24).

Suggested Potential Weaknesses:

1. May have false impulses that are contradictory to God's Word or revelation.
2. Must take extreme care in the case of secrets revealed.
3. Might have a tendency to use acquired knowledge through observation or conversation and reveal it as a Word of Knowledge.
4. Might try to operate on one's own experience of God and His ways rather than supernatural revelation.
5. Can become proud.

3. Gift of Faith

Scriptures: 1 Corinthians 12:9

Greek Usage: *pistis* (SC4102) In general, it implies such a knowledge of, assent to, and confidence in certain divine truths, as produces good works. A miraculous faith.

Various Definitions:

Bruce L. Bugbee: The divine enablement to see the Lord's will and act on it with an unwavering belief in God's ability.[122]

Kevin J. Conner: Special and supernatural faith given by the Spirit for the miraculous.[123]

Frank Damazio: One who can believe God for the impossible; one who has the special gift of faith for what God has promised to do; an ability to see God's promises come to pass.[124]

Leslie B. Flynn: This goes beyond envisioning something that God wants done. It believes that it will be realized despite its unlikeliness, then launches out to accomplish the project in God's name.[125]

R. M. Riggs: Close contact with God, receiving His instructions and letting Him exercise His faith through us.[126]

C. Peter Wagner: The special ability that God gives to some members of the body of Christ to discern with extraordinary confidence the will and purposes of God for the future of His work.[127]

J. Rodman Williams: The gift of faith is a special impartation of faith in God's power and ability to do wonders given by the Holy Spirit and granted to a particular individual for the common good of others. It is an active ministry gift that operates in distinction from the mind. It may be the immediate background for the exercise of gifts of healing and effecting of miracles. It may be a God-given faith in some situations to strengthen the faith of others and give them a special trust in God which reassures them.[128]

Suggested Definition:

The supernatural Manifestation Gift that God gives to certain members of the body of Christ which enables them to discern with extraordinary confidence the will and purposes of God for the future of His work.

Suggested Characteristics:

1. Is more interested in the future than history (Acts 27:25).
2. Is unmoved by circumstances, suffering, or obstacles (Acts 13:46-52).
3. Has great trust in God (Acts 14:8-10).
4. Shows a positive attitude, may be a visionary, dreamer, promoter (Acts 9:27).
5. Is very courageous (Acts 6:5; 7:1-60; 27:25).
6. Senses the moment when "prayer of faith" is needed (Acts 3:1-10).
7. Is goal-centered (Acts 27:25).

Suggested Potential Weaknesses:

1. May be viewed as non-realist because of positive attitudes.
2. May become impatient when others don't have the same kind of positive faith outlook.
3. May have a difficult time understanding "the system" and why it works as it does to slow down progress.
4. May exercise Gift of Faith without works.
5. Is often irritated by criticism because he/she has assurance of knowing God's will.

4. Gifts of Healing

Scriptures: 1 Corinthians 12:9, 28, 30

Greek Usage: *iama* (sc2386) Cure, heal, make whole.

Various Definitions:

Bruce L. Bugbee: The divine enablement to be God's channel to restore people to health.[129]

Kevin J. Conner: Those who have various gifts or a gift of healing by the Spirit, restoring health.[130]

Frank Damazio: One who is used by God as the vessel through which He imparts healing to the physical body at times of His choosing.[131]

Leslie B. Flynn: The ability to intervene in a supernatural way as an instrument for the curing of illness and restoration of health.[132]

R. M. Riggs: Divine enablements to heal the sick apart from the aid of natural means and human skill.[133]

C. Peter Wagner: The special ability that God gives to certain members of the body of Christ to serve as human intermediaries, through whom it pleases God to cure illness and restore health apart from the use of natural means.[134]

J. Rodman Williams: The Gifts of Healings are supernatural endowments which come directly from the Holy Spirit where Jesus is recognized and received as Lord. He freely moves through a particular person to bring about healings. It operates in close connection with the gift of faith.[135]

Suggested Definition:

The supernatural Manifestation Gift that God gives to certain members of the body of Christ which enables them to serve as human intermediaries, through whom it pleases God to cure various illnesses and restore health supernaturally, and is often used in conjunction with the Word of Knowledge and the Gift of Faith.

Suggested Characteristics:

1. Enjoys and senses the need to pray for the healing of the sick (1 Corinthians 14:1; John 5:14-16).
2. Has a great faith that God can heal apart from natural means (Acts 3:6).
3. Has compassion on others who are sick or suffering and is willing to take time in ministering healing to them (Acts 3:6; 9:32-42).
4. Often the gifts of healing come to the person being healed (Paul being healed and then healer).
5. Understands that Jesus is the healer and hence faith is directed away from himself (Acts 3:12).

Suggested Potential Weaknesses:

1. Temptation to pride — boasting after a clear manifestation of the power of God.
2. Tendency to become critical toward others who try to rationalize sickness or who do not believe in God's power to heal.
3. Discouragement if healing does not take place.
4. Temptation to stop listening to God and operate in his own strength or in the flesh.
5. Temptation to doubt God's power, especially with a drastic sickness or illness.
6. Temptation to rush through prayer for the sick and tell the person to "just receive your healing."

5. Gift of Miracles

Scriptures: 1 Corinthians 12:10, 28, 29

Greek Usage: *dunamis* (SC1411) Power, especially inherent power, being able, capable.

Various Definitions:

Bruce L. Bugbee: The divine enablement to effect powerful acts which authenticate the message of Christ and glorify God.[136]

Kevin J. Conner: Works of power, those who do or perform miracles.[137]

Frank Damazio: One who performs what is naturally impossible through the power of God; one who has been gifted with a ministry of power and deliverance.[138]

Leslie B. Flynn: An event of supernatural power, palpable to the senses, accompanying the servant of the Lord to authenticate the divine commission.[139]

R. M. Riggs: A divine ability which when exercised causes an orderly intervention in the regular operations of nature; a supernatural suspension of a natural law.[140]

C. Peter Wagner: The special ability that God gives to certain members of the body of Christ to serve as human intermediaries, through whom it pleases God to perform powerful acts that are perceived by observers to have altered the ordinary course of nature.[141]

J. Rodman Williams: In a broad sense miracles as powers include all demonstrations of supernatural power.[142]

Suggested Definition:

The supernatural Functional Gift that God gives to certain members of the body of Christ which enables them to serve as intermediaries, through whom it pleases God to intervene in the regular operations of nature.

Suggested Characteristics:

1. Often sees supernatural miracles (Acts 5:1-10; 13:8-11).
2. Has a great interest in supernaturalism rather than naturalism (Acts 20:9-12).
3. Is compassionate.
4. Can point to specific instances where his prayers resulted in miracles (Acts 9:32-41).

Suggested Potential Weaknesses:

1. Can be easily abused through selfishness or pride.
2. May feel that everything is OK between him and the Lord because he has done miracles (Matthew. 7:21).

6. Gift of Prophecy

Scriptures: 1 Corinthians 12:8-10

Greek Usage: *propheteia* (SC4393) Speaking forth the mind and counsel of God.

Various Definitions:

Bruce L. Bugbee: The divine enablement to proclaim God's truth with power and clarity in a timely and culturally sensitive fashion for correction, repentance or edification.[143]

Kevin Conner: He who prophesies, a gifted faculty of setting forth inspired utterance in known languages.[144]

Frank Damazio: To occasionally foretell future events; to speak under the inspiration of God's Spirit; a gifted member who inspires, confirms and reinforces revealed truth.[145]

Leslie B. Flynn: The Spirit-given ability to proclaim the written Word of God with clarity and to apply it to a particular situation with a view to correction or edification.[146]

Harold Horton: Supernatural utterance in a known tongue.[147]

R. M. Riggs: To speak for another. Speaking one's own language in the power of the Holy Spirit. Divine ability to forth-tell as well as to fore-tell.[148]

B. E. Underwood: Prophecy is the manifestation of a spontaneously uttered word from the Lord given through any member of the body for the encouragement, edification, or exhortation of the church. This is the one gift that is both a ministry and a manifestation.[149]

C. Peter Wagner: The special ability that God gives to certain members of the body of Christ to receive and communicate an immediate message of God to His people through a divinely-anointed utterance.[150]

J. Rodman Williams: An immediate communication from God in the common language. It is a "speaking forth" by which a person's tongue is completely at the disposal of the Holy Spirit. God communicates in a given situation a special message to His people.[151]

Suggested Definition:

The supernatural Manifestational Gift that God gives to certain members of the body of Christ which enables them to receive and communicate a message from God to man through a divinely-anointed utterance.

Suggested Characteristics:

1. Builds up the community. The whole purpose is positive, although there may be admonition and warning, even exhortation, to desist from some evil. Has a real lifting power and gives real light on the truth to those who hear.
2. Finds consent and agreement in the minds and hearts of others in the community. There should be a prevailing sense in the community that the prophecy was divinely inspired.
3. May be spoken in a variety of ways as the Lord Himself wills it.
4. It comes forth in power of the Spirit of God.
5. Spontaneity marks such an occasion, and the words are divinely inspired.
6. The prophetic word should be given in an orderly manner (1 Corinthians 14:26-40).
7. Not infallible, and the utterance must be judged by the infallible Word of God. The person should be humble enough to allow his word to be judged (1 Corinthians 14:29). If it is the mind of God, there is nothing to fear.
8. Prophecy has a vital connection with faith; the individual must prophesy according to the measure of faith (Romans 12:6).
9. Paul has a tendency to prefer prophecy to other gifts (1 Corinthians 14:1).
10. It stays on the sober ground of faith (cf. Romans 12:6). God gives and the believer makes responsible use of the gifts. Prophecy declares God's counsel openly (1 Corinthians 14:5) and edifies the whole Church, although there may be exhortation and admonition and warning to desist from some evil (14:2-3).
11. It may convict nonbelievers (1 Corinthians 14:24-25).
12. Prophecy should be harmonious with God's Word; it must not take away

from nor add to Scripture, but should intensify and quicken that which already has been given to us from God (1 Corinthians 14:27-33; Revelations 22:19).

13. It may be spoken in a variety of ways; it is the Lord speaking through a human vessel (1 Corinthians 14:3-6, 27-33), in the power of the Holy Spirit (12:4-11).
14. Speaks as one speaking the very words of God (1 Peter 4:10-11).

Suggested Potential Weaknesses:

1. Deals with things that do not edify and are designed to puff up hearers and to lead them into error.
2. If you are not humble enough to allow your prophecy to be judged, it is as surely wrong as you are wrong.
3. If you hear any voices that make you think that you are superior to those whom God has put in the church to rule the church, watch out, for this is surely of the devil.
4. Forgets to praise partial progress (due to goal consciousness).
5. Can be misused if not properly judged (1 Corinthians 14:29).
6. Not all prophecies may be of God (2 Corinthians 11:3-4, 13-15; 2 Thessalonians 2:1-2).
7. The person giving the prophecy may be forbidden or hindered by leaders or the congregation (1 Thessalonians 5:19-20).

7. Gift of Discernment of Spirits

Scriptures: 1 Corinthians 12:10

Greek Usage: *diakrisis* (SC1253) To separate one from another; divide; part; distinguishing.

Various Definitions:

Bruce L. Bugbee: The divine enablement to distinguish between the truth and error.[152]

Kevin J. Conner: To recognize clearly what is the Spirit of God, spirit of error or the human spirit at work. Perception of error or truth.[153]

Leslie B. Flynn: The ability to discriminate between that which is raised up by God and that which pretends to be.[154]

Frank Damazio: One who recognizes what spirit (divine, evil or human) is causing a certain manifestation or activity.[155]

R. M. Riggs: The ability to unmask the deceiving demon and disclose him as an enemy in disguise when needed.[156]

C. Peter Wagner: The special ability that God gives to certain members of the body of Christ to know with assurance whether behavior purported to be of God is in reality divine, human, or satanic.[157]

J. Rodman Williams: It serves particularly to discern the Spirit at work in any expression or activity within the Christian community.[158]

Suggested Definition:

The supernatural Manifestation Gift that God gives to certain members of the body of Christ which enables them to have supernatural insight into the realm of spirits (whether they are of God, Satan, or human).

Suggested Characteristics:

1. Can tell good spirits from evil spirits and right spirits from wrong spirits (1 John 4:1).
2. Can understand the spirits operating (1 Corinthians 14:29; Mark 5:6-13).
3. Can discern the spiritual condition of individuals (Acts 16:16-18).

Suggested Potential Weaknesses:

1. Can be viewed as a suspicion rather than a perception.
2. Tends to be judgmental.
3. To falsely deliver people from spirits could cause more problems than it cures.
4. An *incorrect* judgment of a person by someone assuming he/she has the gift of discernment, (or an understandable mistake by one who legitimately possesses this gift), could cause great harm to that individual and to the body of Christ.
5. Has a tendency to forget using the authority of Jesus' name (Jude 8-10; 2 Peter 2:1-11) and opening the door to spirit activity in his/her own life.
6. May have a "quick fix" mentality regarding evil (Luke 11:24-26).

8. Gift of Tongues

Scriptures: 1 Corinthians 12:10, 28, 30

Greek Usage: *glossa* (SC1100) Tongue, language.

Various Definitions:

Bruce L. Bugbee: The divine enablement to speak in unknown languages.[159]

Kevin J. Conner: A speaker in kinds of tongues, those who speak languages they have never learned, by the Spirit.[160]

Frank Damazio: One who speaks forth a language he does not understand; one who speaks by the Spirit in a language that he has not previously learned.[161]

Leslie B. Flynn: The ability to speak in a foreign language.[162]

R. M. Riggs: The expression of the feelings of God's heart chiefly used in prayer and secondarily as a vehicle of expression for messages to the church.[163]

C. Peter Wagner: The special ability that God gives to certain members of the body of Christ (a) to speak to God in a language they have never learned and/or (b) to receive and communicate an immediate message of God to His people through a divinely-anointed utterance in a language they have never learned.[164]

Suggested Definition:

The supernatural Manifestation Gift that God gives to certain members of the body of Christ which enables them to (a) speak in a language unlearned by the speaker naturally, and/or (b) to receive and communicate an immediate message of God to His people through a divinely-anointed utterance for the interpretation in a language unlearned by the speaker.

Suggested Characteristics:

1. Has publicly spoken in an unlearned language or in ecstatic utterances (Acts 2:4).
2. Speaking in tongues is sometimes directed toward God and is a declaration of praise (1 Corinthians 14:2, 16, 17; Acts 2:11; 10:46).
3. Tongues consist of speaking mysteries in the Spirit (1 Corinthians 14:2).
4. Tongues edify the person doing the speaking (1 Corinthians 14:4,17).
5. The individual must do the speaking, although the Holy Spirit gives the words (Acts 2:4).
6. This gift may be expressed as a form of prayer and also as a way of singing (1 Corinthians 14:14,15; Romans 8:26-27)).
7. The gift consists of "different kinds of tongues" which suggests that there may be a variety of tongues uttered (1 Corinthians 12:10).
8. This gift is a sign to unbelievers (1 Corinthians 14:22).
9. The use of this gift has a strong relationship to the gift of the "interpretation of tongues." For example in the context of a church service:
    a. The one who speaks in a tongue should pray that he may interpret what he says (1 Corinthians 14:13) or know that someone present will be able to interpret or otherwise just speak quietly to God (1 Corinthians 14:28).
    b. It is the accompanying gift of the "interpretation of tongues" that allows the church to be edified (1 Corinthians14:5-19).
    c. Also, tongues and interpretation should be limited to three people and should be done orderly (1 Corinthians 14:27).
10. Tongues *can* also be a sign of the initial reception of the Holy Spirit (Acts 2:4; 10:44-46; 19:6).
11. Tongues as an initial sign of the reception of the Holy Spirit require no interpretation (Acts 2).
12. Interpretation is not required in private use (1 Corinthians 14:14).

13. Tongues as an initial sign (on the Day of Pentecost) are called prophecy (Acts 2:14-18).
14. Singing in the Spirit is meant as singing in tongues (1 Corinthians 14:13-16).
15. Speaking in tongues is sometimes speaking in a known language yet unknown to the speaker (Acts 2:4-6).
16. Has boldness to speak forth.

Suggested Potential Weaknesses:

1. Uncontrolled use and overemphasis can create confusion within local church.
2. Tends to force this gift on others.
3. May be viewed as too much "experience-oriented."

9. Gift of Interpretation

Scriptures: 1 Corinthians 12:10

Greek Usage: *hermeenia* (sc2058) Interpretation.

Various Definitions:

Bruce L. Bugbee: The divine enablement to make known to the Body the message of one who is speaking in tongues.[165]

Kevin J. Conner: To interpret tongues or languages by the power of the Spirit.[166]

Frank Damazio: One who is given supernatural understanding to interpret the meaning of a message in tongues to the Church.[167]

Leslie B. Flynn: The ability to interpret the non-linguistic sounds.[168]

R. M. Riggs: The supernatural ability of interpreting or giving the sense of that which has been spoken in the gift of tongues.[169]

C. Peter Wagner: The special ability that God gives to certain members of the body of Christ to make known in the vernacular the message of one who speaks in tongues.[170]

Suggested Definition:

The supernatural Manifestation Gift that God gives to certain members of the body of Christ which enables them to make known in the vernacular the message of one who speaks in tongues.

Suggested Characteristics:

1. Has interpreted tongues with the result that the body of Christ was edified, exhorted, or comforted (1 Corinthians 14:3, 26).
2. Has sensitivity to the Spirit's promptings; is yielded (1 Corinthians 14:15).
3. Has sensed an understanding of what God is saying while a message in tongues is given (1 Corinthians 14:5).

The following are adapted from J. Rodman Williams:[171]

4. The one interpreting has no more knowledge than the glossolalist of what has been said; the interpreter simply speaks out and the Holy Spirit gives the interpretation.
5. A person must begin to speak in his native language. However, what is said in interpretation is basically from a realm beyond the human mind.
6. The interpretation sometimes varies considerably in length from the tongue spoken. It may be lengthier, or sometimes it may even be shorter, than the incomprehensible utterance.
7. It can bring a powerful message to whomever it is especially addressed (plus supplication and intercession).

Suggested Potential Weaknesses:

1. Seems to be too subjective rather than objective.
2. It is possible that the words of a presumed interpretation are not given by the Holy Spirit (but from human spirit or diabolical spirit).
3. Also it may be that the apparent interpretation is a prophecy.

Gifts Prioritized by God

In the following material we have listed the gifts that are located in the fourth column of the "Most Recognized Classification" — Gifts Prioritized by God. See the previous sections for explanations of these gifts.

1. **Apostolic Gift**
   (see page 32)
2. **Prophetic Gift**
   (see page 35)
3. **Teaching Gift**
   (see page 43)
4. **Gift of Miracles**
   (see page 102)
5. **Gifts of Healing**
   (see page 100)
6. **Gift of Helps/Service**
   (see page 54)
7. **Gift of Administration/Government/Leadership**
   (see page 79)
8. **Gift of Tongues**
   (see page 109)
9. **Gift of Interpretation**
   (see page 112)

Natural Talents

In the following material we have dealt with the gifts listed in the fifth column of the "Most Recognized Classification" — Gifts of God/Natural Talents.

Scriptures: James 1:17

Greek Usage: *didomi* — To give, to bestow, bring forth, commit, deliver or grant.

Various Definitions:

Bruce L. Bugbee: God, in His creative wisdom, has showered His grace on all people. Each person has been granted various talents/abilities/skills as an opportunity to glorify his Creator. Both Christians and unbelievers share in this common grace. Your talents/abilities/skills can be developed through education and experience.[172]

Leslie Flynn: Talents have to do with techniques and methods; gifts have to do with spiritual abilities. Talents depend on natural power, gifts on spiritual endowment. Talents instruct, inspire, or entertain on a natural level. Gifts relate to the building up of the saints. Though natural aptitudes are not spiritual gifts, the Spirit may choose to use our natural powers for the exercise of our God-given gifts.[173]

Ray Stedman: Natural talents deal with the surface areas of life (the natural) whereas spiritual gifts deal with man's spirit — the deepest level of human existence and the root of all human problems. For instance, a person can have a talent for teaching without having the spiritual gift of teaching; the natural talent for teaching may impart knowledge but without the power to bless and strengthen spiritually.[174]

Suggested Definition:

Talents are not gifts of the Spirit. A nonregenerated man has the same talents as a regenerated Spirit-filled man. All people receive these gifts from God. They can be developed and improved by home environment and training. These talents differ from the spiritual gifts (supernaturally endowed) but are more likely to flow as the person matures in his/her faith. This is why Peter urges us to use whatever gifts we have.

Various Characteristics:

Bugbee

Both Natural Talents and Supernatural Gifts:

- Vary in degree and kind.
- Can be developed.
- Are given by God and ought to be used under the Lordship of Jesus Christ (Colossians 3:17, 23, 24).

Natural Talents		*Spiritual Gifts*	
Physical birth		Spiritual birth	
Edifies individual		Edifies others	
Given to all		Given to believers	
Example:	Cooking	Example:	Helps
	Music		Teaching
	Craftsmanship		Giving[175]

NOTE: For each talent there are various characteristics. Therefore, each one should be studied individually.

Spiritual Gifts Discovery

Instructions

The following exercise provides opportunity for you to respond to 105 statements about your interest in, and experience of, spiritual gifts. Do not respond on the basis of what you think you ought to say. Rather, respond on the basis of your interest and your experience. Do not let modesty hinder you from answering honestly about your abilities.

Rate each statement from 0 to 4 based upon your interest and experience. If a statement is not relevant to your experience, answer it by marking a zero (0) in the proper place. Mark a four (4) to indicate a strong tendency.

0 — Not at all

1 — Little

2 — Moderately

3 — Considerably

4 — Strongly

The Gifts Discovery Instrument is a tool, not a final revelation. It is a means to an end, and the end is ministry, i.e., the building up of the body of Christ. The goal of this Instrument is for people to realize their potential in Christ as it relates to building God's Kingdom.

The Instrument can be completed in about 45 minutes. It should be taken when you are in a relatively natural mood — not discouraged, anxious, or overly excited. Above all, the statements should be answered honestly.

After all 105 statements are completed, transfer to the ANSWER SHEET. Then add the five scores across each row, and enter the totals in the appropriate column. Using the results from the ANSWER SHEET, enter the gifts with the three highest scores onto the dominant section of the PERSONAL EVALUATION. Then enter the next three highest scoring gifts onto the subordinate section. This is the tentative evaluation of where your gifts may lie.

For evaluation of the Instrument, there is no set score that determines whether or not you have a particular gift (20 being the highest possible). It is on an individual basis.

For example, if one person's highest scores are 16, 18, 18, 19, and 14, then those would be his/her gift tendencies. However, if someone scored 16, 15, 12, 14, and 10, then those, if they were the person's highest, would be just as valid an indication to that person's gift tendencies as the individual who scored higher.

Spiritual Gifts Discovery Statements

____ 1. I have a desire to commit my life to planting and establishing churches and/or Christian organizations.

____ 2. I have a call from God to give my life full-time to provide spiritual direction to the church and staff out of concern for God's standards.

____ 3. I desire to give my life to winning the unconverted.

____ 4. I desire a position to equip and train a particular group of Christians for the work of the ministry.

____ 5. I tend to be systematic and orderly in studying and presenting truths.

____ 6. I have a sense of what God wants to say to people in response to particular situations.

____ 7. I enjoy devoting considerable time to learning new biblical truths in order to communicate them clearly to others.

____ 8. I tend to see a person's potential, and I have a strong desire to urge people to their full spiritual maturity.

____ 9. I enjoy helping others get their work done, and don't need a lot of public recognition.

____10. When I make a financial contribution, I desire to share in the life and ministry for which my gift is given.

____11. I tend to think futuristically, and organize and plan accordingly.

____12. I am attracted to people who are hurting or in distress.

____13. I have shared insights of spiritual truth which others say helped bring them closer to God.

____14. God enables me to make appropriate application of biblical truth to practical situations.

____15. In specific cases God has given me assurance that He would do what seemed unlikely.

____16. I have had supernatural insight into the spiritual realm.

____17. God has used me to intervene in the ordinary course of nature and see a supernatural consequence.

____18. People seek me out to pray for their healing.

____19. I speak forth words of the Lord that build up the community of believers with exhortation, edification, and comfort.

____20. I have spoken in tongues, as a word from the Lord, expecting it to be interpreted.

____21. I have interpreted tongues which edified, exhorted, or comforted the body of Christ.

____22. I have a burden and vision for the Universal Church, not just the local church.

____23. I have a strong vision for what God wants to do, and I speak about it to people in all levels of leadership.

____24. I enjoy talking about the Lord Jesus to those who do not know Him, and I share the Gospel in a clear and meaningful way to unbelievers.

____25. I enjoy assuming responsibility for the spiritual growth and maturity of a particular group of Christians.

____26. I have a great love for the Word of God, and I desire to teach it accurately.

____27. I sometimes feel I know exactly what God wants to do at a specific point in time.

____28. I enjoy presenting truth in a logical, systematic way.

____29. I love to do personal counseling.

____30. I tend not to care or notice how menial or unpopular a job is. To me it is an act of worship and ministry.

____31. I give cheerfully and liberally, often above what is expected.

____32. I am able to organize ideas, tasks, people, and time effectively..

____33. I have a particular concern for the needs of people, especially spiritually.

____34. I have known facts about people or situations, which were not learned through the efforts of the natural mind.

____35. I have shared spiritual insights on how a given situation, prophecy, or word of knowledge can be applied to a specific situation.

____36. I often discern, with extraordinary confidence, the will and purposes of God for the future of His work.

____37. I have discerned, with a high degree of assurance, when a person is being afflicted by demonic spirits.

____38. I often experience specific instances where my prayers result in miracles.

____39. I enjoy praying for the sick and others needing healing.

____40. People have told me that I have communicated timely and urgent messages which must have come directly from the Lord.

____41. I strongly desire to speak in tongues as a sign to the unbeliever.

____42. When a person speaks in tongues, I get an idea about what God is saying.

____43. I have experienced extraordinary authority in general leadership over a church, churches, or Christian organizations.

____44. I see the need for godly emphasis in programs, stressing in leadership the moral duty to be a good role model, bringing conviction and challenge by my speech and life.

____45. I enjoy training God's people how to proclaim the good news of salvation.

____46. I have a deep concern for discipling individuals by watching over, guiding, and nurturing them.

____47. I desire to teach other teachers valid methods of study, and how to communicate truth to others.

____48. I tend to see things as black or white, true or false, or good or evil.

____49. I love to validate truth by intensive research, and enjoy in-depth study and research.

____50. I am able to identify with all kinds of people, in order to gain a wider acceptance.

____51. I often tend to sense when others need a helping hand, and give it readily.

____52. I have a strong conviction that all I have belongs to God, and I want to be a good steward of His resources.

____53. I have a sense for delegating tasks to the right people at the right time.

____54. I want to help people have right relationships with one another.

____55. The Holy Spirit enables me to reveal to individuals or groups their specific needs.

____56. I have received understanding from God about the best way to handle a situation or problem.

____57. I sense moments when a "prayer of faith" is needed, and many times I am given that "prayer of faith" to pray.

____58. I often sense when angels are present.

____59. God has used me personally to perform supernatural signs and wonders.

____60. God often uses me to bring healing to someone's body.

____61. Through God I have revealed specific things from His point of view, producing liberty to those who receive it.

____62. I have spoken in an unknown language, not previously learned.

____63. I have interpreted a message someone spoke in an unknown language, not previously known to me.

____64. I desire to prepare and appoint other ministries that bring divine order and direction to God's house.

____65. I am open to the Lord to experience personal brokenness and repentance, and to point the whole church in that way, so that God may be glorified.

____66. I have a deep burden for the lost.

____67. I take great delight in restoring people who wander from the right path.

____68. I feel a life-calling to teach and help equip people for service.

____69. My basis for what I believe to be true is founded solely on biblical truth.

____70. I have a tendency to draw applications and illustrations from biblical sources rather than non-biblical ones.

____71. I help those eager to follow steps of action to live victoriously.

____72. I sense great satisfaction from helping others.

____73. I desire to make wise purchases and investments in order to provide more resources for the Lord.

____74. I tend to assume responsibility when no structured leadership exists, and then begin to organize and plan.

____75. I seem to have an extraordinary compassion for those who are in need.

____76. God has given me spiritual insight which strengthened people's faith while I was teaching or giving instruction.

____77. I have received spiritual insight about the person and work of the Lord Jesus Christ, and I share how a specific scripture, teaching, or revelation gives greater understanding.

____78. I am viewed as a "dreamer" because of my positive attitude and strong faith in God.

____79. I often perceive when someone is acting under the influence of a holy spirit, a human spirit, or an evil spirit.

____80. I enjoy reading about the miracles of Jesus and others throughout history, and desire to experience them today.

____81. I have compassion on those who suffer, and desire to be an instrument of God's healing.

____82. I speak forth words that give clarity to truth that has already been given.

____83. I have a desire to hear God speak to the Church through tongues.

____84. I have a great desire to interpret what God speaks to the church through tongues.

____85. I like to form teams that will work with me.

____86. It is evident in my life that beside the gift of prophecy, other revelation gifts such as: Discerning of Spirits, Word of Wisdom, or the Word of Knowledge are activated in my life so that I am recognized as a leader in the church.

____87. I desire to preach the Gospel, and be used in leading many people to the Lord.

____88. I would enjoy relating to a certain group of people over a long period of time, sharing personally in their successes and their failures.

____89. I see people looking to me to clarify sound doctrine.

____90. I tend to perceive things directly, from within my spirit. I can't always give an explanation of how I know, some might call it intuitive.

____91. I am concerned that the truth be presented in its complete context and am disturbed when scripture is used out of context.

____92. I love to recommend precise steps of action which aid personal growth.

____93. I enjoy serving people, knowing that I am a blessing to them and the Lord.

____94. I enjoy giving to meet needs, without pressure of appeals, whether my giving is public knowledge or not.

____95. I usually desire to start a new challenge when a previous task is completed.

____96. I tend to lack firmness with people unless I can see how it will benefit them.

____97. At times the Holy Spirit enables me to declare truth totally beyond my natural capacity or experience to strengthen the body of Christ.

____98. I often sense a keen awareness of how to pray or respond to particular needs.

____99. I tend to have great and unswerving trust in God and His promises.

____100. I observe the Spirit of God resting on certain people from time to time.

____101. I have great interest in the supernatural and God's almighty, miraculous power.

____102. I often sense a need for healing in someone and sense the faith to be healed.

____103. I tend to speak forth those things I believe in a bold, direct, and persuasive manner.

____104. I have noticed that when I speak in tongues, as a message from the Lord to the body of Christ, it is different from my private prayer language.

____105. When I interpret someone speaking in tongues, as a message from the Lord to the body of Christ, I sense the message comes from beyond my own human mind.

Spiritual Gifts Discovery Answer Sheet

Name ______________________________ Date ____________

Answers					Total	Gift
1____	22____	43____	64____	85____	______	Apostolic Leadership
2____	23____	44____	65____	86____	______	Prophetic Leadership
3____	24____	45____	66____	87____	______	Evangelistic Leadership
4____	25____	46____	67____	88____	______	Pastoral Leadership
5____	26____	47____	68____	89____	______	Teacher Leadership
6____	27____	48____	69____	90____	______	Prophecy
7____	28____	49____	70____	91____	______	Teaching
8____	29____	50____	71____	92____	______	Encouragement
9____	30____	51____	72____	93____	______	Helps/Service
10____	31____	52____	73____	94____	______	Giving
11____	32____	53____	74____	95____	______	Administration
12____	33____	54____	75____	96____	______	Showing Mercy
13____	34____	55____	76____	97____	______	Word of Knowledge
14____	35____	56____	77____	98____	______	Word of Wisdom
15____	36____	57____	78____	99____	______	Faith
16____	37____	58____	79____	100____	______	Discerning of Spirits
17____	38____	59____	80____	101____	______	Miracles
18____	39____	60____	81____	102____	______	Healing
19____	40____	61____	82____	103____	______	Prophecy
20____	41____	62____	83____	104____	______	Tongues
21____	42____	63____	84____	105____	______	Interpretation

Spiritual Gifts Discovery Personal Evaluation

Name____

Using the results in the TOTAL column from the ANSWER SHEET, the gifts with the:

- *Three highest* scores are considered your **Dominant Gift Tendencies**
- *Next three highest* are considered your **Subordinate Gift Tendencies**

I. According to this instrument, my dominant gift tendencies are:

1. ______________________________
2. ______________________________
3. ______________________________

II. According to this instrument, my subordinate gift tendencies are:

1. ______________________________
2. ______________________________
3. ______________________________

III. I now use the six gifts listed above in the body of Christ by:

1. ______________________________
2. ______________________________
3. ______________________________

IV. I welcome an opportunity to begin to use the above gifts which I am not using:

1. ______________________________
2. ______________________________
3. ______________________________

Spiritual Gifts Discovery Practical Steps

C. Peter Wagner:[176]

1. **Prerequisites**
   a. You have to be a Christian.
   b. You have to believe in spiritual gifts.
   c. You have to be willing to work.
   d. You have to pray.
2. **Explore the Possibilities**
   a. Study the Bible.
   b. Learn your church's position on gifts.
   c. Read extensively.
   d. Get to know gifted people.
   e. Make gifts a conversation piece.
3. **Experiment with as Many Gifts as Possible**

   Be available for any job around the church you might be asked to do. When you get an assignment, undertake it in prayer. Ask the Lord to show you through that experience whether you might have a spiritual gift along those lines.
4. **Examine Your Feelings**

   "Christians grow beyond shallow concepts of discipleship that equate unhappiness with serving God."[177] It is the same God who gives spiritual gifts who also oversees the way each one of us is made up in our total being.

5. **Evaluate Your Effectiveness**

Since the spiritual gifts are task-oriented, it is not out of order to expect them to work. If God has given you a gift, He has done so because He wants you to accomplish something for Him in the context of the body of Christ.

6. **Expect Confirmation From the Body**

If you think you have a spiritual gift and are trying to exercise it, but no one else in your church thinks you have it — you probably don't. It needs to be confirmed.

Importance of Knowing Your Spiritual Gifts

Kenneth C. Kinghorn:[178]

Sometimes the question is asked, "Can spiritual gifts operate through me if I am not aware of my spiritual gifts?" The answer is, "Of course they can." Most assuredly, one can manifest spiritual gifts without understanding or even being aware of them.

However, there are many good reasons for our knowing and understanding our gifts. We stand in a much more favorable position to become effective disciples when we identify and develop the spiritual gifts God has given us. Specifically, here are some solid reasons for you to become aware of your spiritual gifts:

1. **Helps you determine God's will for your vocation.**
   A knowledge of your gifts will provide a context for making career and ministry decisions regarding what *not* to attempt as well as what to enter into with confidence.
2. **Mobilizes the entire church for mission.**
   Since a small percentage of the church consists of clergy and more than ninety percent of the church consists of non-clergy, the church obviously must equip and encourage every Christian to minister in his or her respective sphere or influence.
3. **Assists you in setting priorities for study, growth, and ministry.**
   Since each of us has a limited amount of time to develop our potential, it seems clear that we should develop ourselves in the areas of our special gifts.
4. **Gives each Christian a sense of dignity and self worth.**
   Every Christian is an important part of the total church. There are no "second Class" citizens in the Christian community because each person constitutes a vitally significant member of the body of Christ.

5. **Enables you to receive the gift ministries of others.**

   When Christians become more knowledgeable of their own spiritual gifts and those of other Christians, they can more easily function harmoniously as the body of Christ, both giving and receiving ministries.

6. **Fosters unity among fellow Christian believers.**

   As the members of the church function inter-dependently (not independently), an awareness of spiritual gifts leads them to respect one another as they live together in the common life of the Spirit. The application of spiritual gifts is where the rubber meets the road. Spiritual gifts discovery without application is to render powerless the ability God has given us to build His Kingdom.

Spiritual Gifts Discovery Career Applications

The following is a practical guide for matching spiritual gifts to possible Church ministries. While this list is not comprehensive, it offers a broad spectrum of possibilities. You can help members find their place of ministry by looking up their spiritual gift from the following list.

1. Apostolic Leadership Gift

Train and Discipline Ministries	Church Planter
Pastor (administrator)	Missionary
Establish Local Churches	Outreach
Ordain Elders	Organization
Staff Ministries	Teaching

2. Prophetic Leadership Gift

Boards and Committees	Missionary
Outreach	Preaching
Pastoral Staff	Vision
Pastor	Music

3. Evangelistic Leadership Style

Outreach	Visitation
Crusade Preaching	Altar Counselor
Telephoning Prospects	Rescue Mission
Door-to-Door Visitation	Prison Ministry
Training Evangelists	Pastor (Outreach)
Evangelistic Bible Study Leader	Foreign Exchange Student Host
Friend to International Student	Greeter
Prison/Jail Visitation	Stephen Minister

4. Pastor/Shepherd (Functioning in Shepherding Style)

Home Bible Study Leader	Discipleship
Visitation	Outreach
Training	Follow-up

Youth Work
Counseling
Pastor (Counseling)
Premarital Counselor
Stephen Minister
Telecare Coordinator/Member
Children's Work
Cell Groups
Intercessory Prayer Group Coord.
Prison/Jail Visitation
Sunday School Teacher

5. Teacher (Functioning in a Teaching Style)

Children's Sunday School Teacher
Discipleship
Home Bible Study Leader
Visitation
Adult Sunday School Teacher
Pastor (teaching)
Teaching Teachers to Teach
Board Member
Outreach
Youth Worker
Camp Speaker
Minister of Education
Children's Church Leader

6. Gift of Prophecy

Shares a "word" from God
Adult Sunday School Teacher
Music
Boards and Committees
Vision Making
Prison/Jail Visitation
Stephen Minister
Outreach
Cell Groups
Preaching
Evangelism
Intercessory Prayer Group
Spiritual Gifts Advisor
Youth Leader

7. Gift of Teaching

Sunday School Teacher
Home Bible Study Leader
Youth Worker
Visitations
Board Member
Outreach
Discipleship
Recreation Director
Singles Ministry
Camp Speaker

8. Gift of Encouragement

Adult Sunday School Teacher
Children's Sunday School Worker
Discipleship
Greeter

- Boards and Committees
- Vacation Bible School Teacher
- Camp Counselor
- Leading Worship
- Hospital Visitation
- Home Visitation
- Bond Sales/Funds Solicitor
- Corresponder to Missionaries
- Deacon/Deaconess
- Evangelism Committee
- Friend to International Student
- Intercessory Prayer Group Coord.
- Landscaping Supervisor
- Music Coordinator
- Premarital Counselor
- Singles Ministry Coordinator
- Sports Coordinator/Coach
- Sunday School Coordinator
- Youth Leader/Sponsor/Worker
- Visitation
- Counseling
- Usher
- Prayer Ministry
- Altar Worker
- Bible Club Coordinator
- Choir Coordinator/ Director
- Dance Team Director
- Drama Team Member/Director
- Foreign Exchange Student Host
- Information Booth Worker/Coord.
- Kitchen Coordinator
- Men's Ministry Coordinator
- Orchestra/Band Director
- Prison/Jail Visitation
- Small Group Coordinator/Leader
- Stephen Minister
- Women's Ministry Coordinator
- Young Couple Coordinator

9. Gifts of Helps/Service

- Tape Ministry
- Advertising
- Boys Club (Scout Troops)
- Girls Club (Scout Troops)
- Organ, Piano, other instruments
- Seniors Fellowship
- Choir, Ensemble
- Musician
- Recreation Director
- Handyman/Building Maintenance
- Crafts
- Committees
- Bible Study Leader
- Church Bulletin
- Children's Sunday School Teacher
- Men's Fellowship
- Teacher's Aide
- Photographer
- Parking Lot
- Back Yard Bible
- Mechanic
- Media Committee
- Church Office Worker
- Children's Work

Bus Driver/Van Driver
Camp
Nursery
Cooking
Library
Kid's Club Activities
Helping with Mail-outs
Communion Preparation
Sunday School Secretary
New Infant Recognition
Church Building Repair
Sunday School Class Officer
Church Security Worker
Corresponder to Missionaries
Deacon/Deaconess
Info Booth Worker/Coordinator
Overhead Projectionist
Publicity Facilitator
Shut-In Visitation Coordinator
Audio/Visual Technician
Telephoning
Hospital Visitation
Baptism Preparation
Church Landscape
Transportation
Children's Music
Arts and Crafts
Greeter
Women's Ministries
Drama
Usher
Flower Arranging
Coffee Time Host/Hostess
Dance Team Member
Evangelism Committee Member
Meal Coordinator
Prison/Jail Visitation
Refreshment Coordinator
Youth Sponsor
Friend to International Student

10. Gift of Giving

Boards and Committees
Meals and Lodging
Support Missionaries
Fund Raiser
Benevolent Ministries
Giving Above the Tithe
Finance/Management Committee
Church Treasurer
Sponsor Students
Build Buildings
Help the Needy
Missions
Relief Agencies

11. Gift of Administration, Government, Leadership

Organize Special Events
Activities Coordinator
Sunday School Superintendent
Library
Adult Ed. Committee Member
Cell Groups

- Boards and Committees
- Leadership Training
- General Administration
- Church Office Work
- Sunday School Class Officer
- Vacation Bible Coordinator
- Bond Sales/Funds Solicitor
- Communion Preparer
- Drama Team Director
- Finance Comm. Member/Chair
- Information Booth Coordinator
- Kitchen Coordinator
- Men's Ministry Coordinator
- Music Librarian
- Orchestra/Band Director
- Publicity Facilitator
- Singles Ministry Coordinator
- Telecare Coordinator
- Women's Ministry Coordinator
- Young Couples Coordinator
- Deacon/Deaconess
- Camp Director
- Church Historian
- Recruiter
- Financial Secretary
- Head Usher
- Bible Club Coordinator
- Choir Director
- Dance Team Director
- Evangelism Comm. Member/Chair
- Hospital Visitation Coordinator
- Intercessory Prayer Group Coord.
- Media Ministry Member/Coordinator
- Missions Committee Chairperson
- Office Assistant
- Prayer Chain Phone Member/Coord.
- Secretary/Treasurer
- Summer Camp Director
- Worship Leader
- Youth Leader/Sponsor
- Landscaping Supervisor
- Small Group Coordinator/Leader

12. Gift of Showing Mercy

- Altar Counselor
- Divorce Recovery
- Drug and Alcohol
- Abused Children
- Shut-in Ministry
- Prison Ministry
- Evangelism/Soul Winner
- Bereaved Ministry
- Cancer Care
- Nursery Worker
- Premarital Counselor
- Mentally Ill Ministry
- Hospital Visitation
- Convalescent Homes
- Missions Work
- Deaf Ministry
- Singles Ministry
- Blind Ministry
- Outreach
- Deacon/Deaconess
- Prayer Chain Member/Coordinator
- Stephen Minister

13. Word of Knowledge

Boards and Committees
Research
Youth Worker
Marriage Enrichment
Committee Member
Visitation
Spiritual Gifts Advisor
Ability to share "a word" of insight from God otherwise impossible to know
Altar Counselor
Teaching
Counseling
Bible Translation
Discipleship
Deacon/Deaconess
Stephen Minister

14. Word of Wisdom

Boards and Committees
Research
Youth Worker
Marriage Enrichment
Counseling
Deacon/Deaconess
Intercessory Prayer Group Coord.
Premarital Counselor
Ability to counsel people about situations with supernatural insight
Bible Translation
Visitation
Discipleship
Altar Counselor
Teaching
Evangelism Committee Member
Missions Committee Member
Spiritual Gifts Advisor
Stephen Minister

15. Gift of Faith

Prayer Ministries
Nominating Committee
Altar Counselor
Building Projects
Fund Raising
Evangelism Committee Chairperson
Prayer Chain Leader/Member
Board Member
Healing Ministry
Prayer Partner
Hospital Visitation
Deacon/Deaconess
Intercessory Prayer Group Member

16. Gift of Discernment of Spirits

Board Member
Evangelism

Recruiter
Altar Counselor
Counseling
Visitation
Divorce/Recovery
Youth Work
Adult Education Committee Member
Deacon/Deaconess
Intercessory Prayer Group
Prayer Chain Member
Premarital Counselor
Prison/Jail Visitation
Stephen Minister
Worship Leader

17. Gift of Miracles

Healing Ministries
Prayer Ministries
Anointing of Believers
Missions Work
Hospital Visitation
Altar Work

18. Gifts of Healing

Healing Ministries
Prayer Ministries
Missions Work
Altar Work
Visitation

19. Prophecy

Adult Education Teacher
Evangelism Team Member/Leader
Evangelistic Bible Study Leader
Instrumentalist
Intercessory Prayer Group
Preaching
Prison/Jail Visitation
Small Group Leader
Spiritual Gifts Advisor
Stephen Minister
Sunday School Teacher
Worship/Ensemble Singer
Worship Leader
Youth Leader

20. Gifts of Tongues

Worship Leader
Missions
Prayer Ministries
Board Member
Uses a worship service to share God's message

21. Gift of Interpretation

Worship Leader
Missions
Board Member
Prayer Ministries
Interpretation of Tongues in Worship

Recruiting Effective Volunteers[179]

Kenneth Gangel in his work *Feeding and Leading* gives us the following helpful guidelines involving and training the laity.

A. Introduction

1. A survey which appeared in *Leadership* journal, 1982, said that motivating and sustaining active participation of lay members is the most frustrating problem pastors face today.
2. "The more members that become involved in church ministry roles, the easier it is to find the right persons best qualified and gifted for a particular ministry."
3. Most churches already contain within congregational ranks more than enough potential leaders if gift and call were activated.
4. Three things we do *not* practice in effective recruiting:
    a. General public announcements
    b. Last-minute appointments
    c. Pressurized appeals

B. Determine High Standards

Four areas ought to concern every Christian leader looking for potential volunteer workers either in the local church or in para church ministries:

1. Spiritual Maturity

    What we mean by spiritual maturity may vary from church to church, but the standards you develop should clearly be supported by the Word of God.

2. Leadership Skills
    a. Springer suggests at least three qualities of people with leadership skills:
        1) the ability to win the respect of others

2) the ability to gain people's trust

3) the ability to take the initiative

b. American Association of School Administrators suggests:

1) Is the candidate reputable as a person and as a public worker and recognized by the intelligent leaders of the community?

2) Does she/he have personal courage, exercised with appropriate tact, in facing opposition?

3) Is the candidate likely to avoid fanfare and self-publicity in this post?

4) Does the candidate have the ability to deal democratically and effectively with employees?

5) Is this candidate one who has propensity for keeping his feet on the ground, willing to recognize legitimate precedent, yet also willing to consider appropriate change?

3. Learning Potential

Potential leaders tend to be organized people who understand goals and priorities.

C. Expect Ministry Involvement

1. Volunteers are not members of the staff.
2. Volunteers are not full-time workers.
3. Volunteers cannot be taken for granted.
4. Volunteers are not paid.
5. Volunteers are not bound to a job in the church for long periods of time.

D. Develop Effective Servants

1. Match Persons and Positions
2. Follow Proven Procedures

a. Start early — enlistment should take place at least three months before the person actually begins serving in order to allow time for orientation and training.

b. Make all contacts face-to-face if possible. Sometimes a phone call may be necessary, but direct conversation is much better.

c. Have your information in hand. Know the experience, gifts, and interests of the potential volunteer so you can genuinely affirm the committee's selection in light of the best information available.

d. Anticipate excuses.

e. Assure him of your help and prayer.

3. Specify Persons, Tasks, and Time

Ask specific people for a specific ministry for a specific length of time.

4. Give a job description with an end date.

E. Content and Skills of the Training Program

1. Learn From Biblical Models

a. Contrast between Joshua 1 and Judges 1 shows what happens when a leader trains a successor and what happens when he does not. Moses to Joshua smooth.

b. Elijah to Elisha similar flow.

c. Jesus called and taught the Twelve.

2. Helpful Questions to Assess the Strengths and Weaknesses of Current Training Procedures:

a. What are the current ways you use to train your leaders?

b. Whom do you spend most of your time training?

c. What are the results of that time spent?

d. Who needs to be trained?

e. How do those responsible for the training of leaders relate procedurally to the people who need to be trained?

f. How do those who need to be trained participate in the learning experiences?

g. Under what limitations are you performing the task of training those whom we want to reach?

h. To what extent do present training procedures help to reach those whom we want to reach?

i. How do these procedures need to be improved?

j. What will be the time and type of the training programs?

3. Time and Type of the Training Programs

a. It is related to the age-level taught.

b. It is practical.

c. It is related to the curriculum taught.

d. It is experiential.

e. It is regular and systematic.

Making It Easy to Teach the Gifts

A Way to Teach Spiritual Gifts in Ten Weeks

Many pastors teach Spiritual Gifts in their pastor's class, or adult and Sunday school teachers have taught the material in their respective classes. What the following material includes is the *Suggested Definitions, Common Characteristics,* and *Potential Weaknesses* of each gift. It does not deal with all of the various authors' *Suggested Weaknesses, Common Characteristics,* etc. The students would have to study that for themselves.

It is suggested that the teacher of the material understand the introduction and classification of the gifts in this book, and they should give an overview of these to the class.

Week One
Introduction and Apostolic Gift

Introduction to the Spiritual Gifts

1. Gifts from God the Father (Romans 12)
2. Gifts from the Holy Spirit (1 Corinthians12-14)
3. Gifts from the Son (Ephesians 4)

1. Apostolic Gift

Biblical Example: Paul

Suggested Definition:

The special supernatural Ascension Gift, differing from the 12 apostles (pre-Ascension), that God gives to certain members of the body of Christ to assume and exercise general leadership over and equip the Church with an extraordinary authority in spiritual matters. The Apostolic gift active in the church today is one that is manifested in people who have been given a spiritual authority to gather others in the work of the Lord, normally to start churches or establish order in or build existing ones.

Suggested Characteristics:

1. Will have *spiritual authority* from God in order to guide workers in their service of the Lord (Acts 16:1-4,9,10; 17:15; 20:3-5,13,14; 1 Corinthians 16:10-12; 8:6; 2 Corinthians 8:16-18).
2. Is willing to *devote his life* to planting and establishing the church (1 Thessalonians 2:7).
3. Will be involved in *founding and/or establishing* churches, programs or ministries (1 Corinthians 5:1-13; 2 Corinthians 2:6-11).
4. Will preach and teach the Word (1 Timothy 2:7; 2 Timothy 1:11).
5. Will prepare, ordain, and appoint other ministries (Acts 6:1-6; 16:1-4).
6. Will be involved in implementing Church discipline (Matthew 18:15-17; 1 Corinthians 4:21; Acts 15; 2 Thessalonians 3:14).
7. Will have a vision for the whole body of Christ (Ephesians 3:1-9; 4:1-16).
8. Will organize God's house in Divine order (1 Corinthians 11:34; 7:17; 16:1-2).
9. May have a sense of calling to a particular people or group (Galatians 2:8).
10. Will tend to form teams that will work with him (Acts 16:9; 18:2-24; 19:24).
11. Senses God's direction for the Church.
12. Has a burden for the Church universally (2 Corinthians 11:28).
13. Is more concerned for God's plan than individual needs.
14. Focuses on spiritual growth of groups more than of individuals.

Suggested Potential Weaknesses:

1. Lacks ability to concentrate long on one area; lacks longevity.
2. Is program- rather than people-oriented.
3. Lacks one-on-one ability.
4. Tends to be authoritarian.

Suggested Uses:

1. Church planter
2. Pastor
3. Ministry director
4. Organizer and Administrator
5. Program director
6. Outreach
7. Teaching

Week Two

Prophetic (Equipping) and Evangelistic Gifts

2. Prophetic Gift

Biblical Example: Agabus in Acts

Suggested Definition:

The special supernatural Ascension Gift differing from the pre-Ascension prophets that God gives to certain members of the body of Christ to represent God before the Church as a spokesman and equipping agent, to present the heart, will, and purpose of God in forth telling or foretelling.

Suggested Characteristics:

1. Has strong desire to speak forth the truth, especially as it pertains to right and wrong, good and evil; will include exhortation, reproof, warning, edification, and comfort (Acts 15:32; 1 Corinthians 14:3; Ephesians 5:11; Jeremiah 20:9).
2. Is concerned for reputation of God and the fulfillment of His program (John 2:13-17).
3. Has a strong vision for what God wants to do and declares it clearly to men (Ephesians 3:1-5).
4. Is extremely bold; does not mince words (Luke 3:7ff; Galatians 2:11ff).
5. Focuses on spiritual growth of groups more than individuals; has a concern for the corporate holiness of God's people, desiring them to be truly set apart by their lifestyle, values, and relationships (Matthew 5-7; Revelation 2-3).
6. Confirms direction (Acts 13:1-3).
7. Has an integral part in establishing the foundations of the Church (Ephesians 2:20-22).
8. Experiences much brokenness in his life; identifies with the sins and failings of God's people (Isaiah 22:4; Jeremiah 4:19; 8:21ff).

9. His life is characterized by great spiritual intensity and discipline; spends much time in prayer and fasting (Luke 2:26-37).
10. Often uses the gifts of the Word of Knowledge and Word of Wisdom (Acts 21:10-11).
11. May have a desire to write down the declarations of God's heart (1 Thessalonians. 5:19-20).
12. On occasions can predict national events as well as personal destinies (Acts 5:1-11; 11:27-30; 21:8-14).
13. Often suffers rejection because of his word and is not duly honored (Matthew 13:57; 23:34; Luke 4:24; Revelation 11).
14. Has a life calling to ministering to the body of Christ.

Suggested Potential Weaknesses:

1. Tends to be judgmental and blunt, and dwells on the negative (Jonah 3:4).
2. Frankness may be viewed as harshness (Galatians 1:6-9; 5:7-12).
3. Tends to condemn self when there is failure to evoke the right response in others (Jeremiah 20:7-18).
4. Tends to take on responsibility which is not rightfully his own (Romans 14:4).
5. If self is too strong (pride) and there is a lack of sober self-assessment (humility, purity), the danger is great to be deceived and to deceive others in turn (Jeremiah 23; Ezekiel 13; 2 Peter 2).
6. Because of tendency to be excessively critical, needs to consciously develop attitudes of mercy and patience (Romans 9:1-3; 1 Thessalonians 5:14).
7. Neither his utterances nor his writings are to be considered as normative or infallible; his words must be judged by the Word of God (1 Corinthians 14:29, 30).
8. His manner of expression is very authoritative and at times even negative (Acts 21:10-12; 2 Corinthians 13:2-3; 1 Thessalonians 4:8).

Suggested Uses:

1. Sharing a word from God
2. Intercession
3. Spiritual gifts advisor
4. Prison and jail ministries
5. Inner city ministry
6. Ministry at the altar
7. Ministry in cell groups
8. Boards and committees

3. Evangelistic Gift

Biblical Example: Philip

Suggested Definition:

The special supernatural Ascension Gift that God gives to certain members of the body of Christ to both proclaim the Good News of salvation with extraordinary effectiveness and to equip God's people in their personal and corporate soul-winning efforts.

Suggested Characteristics:

1. Enjoys talking about Jesus to the lost (Acts 8:5).
2. Is very instrumental in leading others to believe in Christ as Savior (2 Timothy 4:5).
3. Has a burden for the lost (Romans 9:1-3).
4. Enjoys being with unbelievers in order to share the gospel (Acts 8:25).
5. Is able to persuade people to make decisions (2 Corinthians 5:14-15).
6. Is able to sense when a person does not know Jesus Christ, and to have compassion for that person (Acts 8:34-35).
7. Feels a life calling into the evangelistic ministry.

Suggested Potential Weaknesses:

1. Is judgmental towards others who are not involved in evangelism (Luke 9:45-46).
2. Relies on own power of expression or persuasion to convert people (1 Corinthians 2:1-5).
3. Because emphasis is on winning the lost, could be viewed as lacking spiritual depth.

Suggested Uses:

1. Outreach to the lost
2. In charge of telephoning prospects
3. In charge of greeters
4. In charge of visitation
5. Training soul winners

Week Three

Pastoral/Leadership and Teacher (Equipping) Gifts

4. Pastoral/Leadership

Good Biblical Example: Timothy

Suggested Definition:

The special supernatural Ascension Gift that God gives to certain members of the body of Christ to equip and care for the spiritual well-being of the flock of God.

Suggested Characteristics:

1. Assumes responsibility for tender care and vigilant superintendence.
2. Enjoys one-to-one discipling and caring.
3. Assumes responsibility when he sees a Christian being led astray.
4. Is able to watch over, guide, train, and nurture other believers toward spiritual maturity and work of the ministry.
5. Senses a shepherding (caring) instinct.
6. Enjoys training saints for the work of ministry.
7. Has personal experience of affliction — God comforts us that we may comfort others (2 Corinthians 1:4).
8. Has ability to give empathetic and undivided attention to someone in need — to set aside one's own interests and concerns in order to be more fully present to one who is suffering (Philippians 2:5-7).
9. Empathizes.
10. Shows vulnerability — "wounded healer."
11. Is able to maintain confidentiality.
12. Desires to comfort those who are ill or grieving and to help them find Christ as the center of their lives.
13. Desires to help others to be healed of past hurts through forgiveness and prayer.

14. Desires to help others resolve issues concerning belief, doubt, sin, guilt (true and false), and life's meaning.
15. Feels a call into full-time ministry of caring.

Suggested Potential Weaknesses:

1. Becomes overly involved with individuals at the expense of the group.
2. Tends to have narrow vision of local ministry rather than corporate.
3. May lack organizational abilities.
4. In an effort to disciple, neglects evangelism.
5. May foster dependency in the one being helped.
6. May feel powerless if unable to provide specific solutions to another's suffering.
7. May not discern another's need for more professional help with problems.

Suggested Uses:

1. In charge of pastoral care
2. Outreach to the hurting
3. Visitation of the flock
4. Follow-up of visitors

5. Teaching Gift

Biblical Example: Peter and John the Baptist

Suggested Definition:

The special supernatural Ascension Gift that God gives to certain members of the body of Christ to present God's Word in a manner that displays spiritual authority and unusual, accurate promoting of health and maturity, while equipping individual members and the body itself for the work of ministry.

Suggested Characteristics:

1. Tends to be systematic (Acts 20:20, 27).
2. Enjoys studying the Word and doing research (Ezra 7:10).
3. Is a good communicator (Acts 18:24-26).
4. Is responsible for teaching other teachers (2 Timothy 2:2).
5. Has a desire to teach, to pass on truth and information (Romans 1:11; Colossians 1:28,29).
6. Tends to be concerned with details; strives for accuracy of content and expression (Acts 17:11).
7. Tends to work well in teacher-student relationships (Luke 19:47,48; 21:37-38).
8. Tends to be orderly in presentation (Nehemiah 8:7-8).
9. Has a life calling to teaching the body of Christ.

Suggested Potential Weaknesses:

1. By reason of his ministry, appeals to reason, understanding, and logic, and may lack emotional appeal.
2. Tends toward being legalistic and dogmatic.
3. Shows too much concern about head knowledge and too little concern with heart knowledge.
4. Is more concerned about content of teaching than person being taught.
5. Gives the impression that he or she is the only source of faith.
6. May not live by his/her own teaching.
7. Has the ability to make the Word say whatever he/she wants it to say.
8. May teach certain doctrines to an extreme.
9. May not incorporate enough practical creativity in teaching, and therefore must fight dullness.
10. May become unteachable if pride gets in the way.

Suggested Uses:

1. Music
2. Outreach
3. Vision-making
4. Preaching

Week Four

Prophecy (Functional) and Helps/Service Gifts

6. Gift of Prophecy

Biblical Example: Peter and John the Baptist

Suggested Definition:

The supernatural Functional Gift that God gives to certain members of the body of Christ which enables them to act often as one in the office of a prophet, but without a life calling to be a minister. They often receive and communicate a message from God to mankind through a divinely anointed utterance.

Suggested Characteristics:

1. Has a burden to share God's Word to the body.
2. Harmonizes with God's own Word in Scripture (the same Spirit speaks). Never takes from nor adds to the Scriptures, but will intensify and quicken that which already has been given to us of God. Brings forth things new and old out of the Scriptures of truth and will make them living and powerful to us.
3. Builds up the community. The whole purpose is positive, although there may be admonition and warning, even exhortation, to desist from some evil. Has a real lifting power and gives real light on the truth to those who hear.
4. Finds consent and agreement in the minds and hearts of others in the community. There should be a prevailing sense in the community that the prophecy was divinely inspired.
5. May be spoken in a variety of ways as the Lord Himself wills it.
6. It comes forth in power of the Spirit of God.
7. Spontaneity marks such an occasion, and the words are divinely inspired.
8. The prophetic word should be given in an orderly manner (1 Corinthians 14:31-33).

9. Not infallible, and the utterance must be judged by the infallible Word of God. The person should be humble enough to allow his word to be judged (1 Corinthians 14:29). If it is the mind of God, there is nothing to fear.
10. Prophecy has a vital connection with faith; the individual must prophesy according to the measure of faith (Romans 12:6).
11. It stays on the sober ground of faith (cf. Romans 12:6). God gives, and the believer makes responsible use of the gifts. Prophecy declares God's counsel openly (1 Corinthians 14:5) and edifies the whole Church, although there may be exhortation and admonition and warning to desist from some evil (14:2-3).

Suggested Potential Weaknesses:

1. Deals with things that do not edify and are designed to puff up hearers and lead them into error.
2. If you are not humble enough to allow your prophecy to be judged, it is as surely wrong as you are wrong.
3. If you hear any voices that make you think that you are superior to those whom God has put in the Church to rule the Church, watch out, for this is surely of the devil.
4. Forgets to praise partial progress (due to goal consciousness).
5. Can be misused if not properly judged (1 Corinthians 14:29).
6. Not all prophecies may be of God (2 Corinthians 11:3-4, 13-15; 2 Thessalonians 2:1-2).
7. The person giving the prophecy may be forbidden or hindered by leaders or the congregation (1 Thessalonians 5:19-20).

Suggested Uses:

1. Sharing a word from God
2. Intercession
3. Spiritual gifts advisor
4. Prison and jail ministries
5. Inner city ministry
6. Ministry at the altar
7. Ministry in cell groups
8. Boards and committees

7. Gift of Helps/Service

Biblical Example: Martha and Timothy

Suggested Definition:

The supernatural Functional Gift that God gives to certain members of the body of Christ which enables them to invest their talents and available resources in the life and/or ministry of another in a manner that helps others accomplish their goals.

Suggested Characteristics:

1. Readily recognizes practical needs and is quick to meet those needs.
2. Feels a deep joy in serving, especially when it releases others to get more involved in their ministry (Romans 16:1-2).
3. Has a keen memory, remembering people's likes and dislikes.
4. Will stay with a project until it is completed. Perfectionist.
5. Is more interested in meeting needs of others than in own needs.
6. Enjoys working on projects with immediate goals instead of long-range goals; wants to see a job finished.
7. Would rather serve than lead others or projects.

Suggested Potential Weaknesses:

1. May become pushy or interfering in own eagerness to help.
2. May neglect own family's needs by being too busy helping others.
3. May be critical of others who do not detect and meet obvious needs.
4. Finds it hard to accept being served by others.
5. Is easily hurt when unappreciated.
6. Can become overly occupied with much serving, even overlooking personal health.
7. Has real difficulty in saying "no."

Suggested Uses:

Any area that needs help, including:

1. Parking lot
2. Tape ministry
3. Church bulletins
4. Media committee
5. Church office
6. Sunday school

Week Five

Teaching (Functional) Exhortation/Encouragement Gifts

8. Gift of Teaching

Suggested Definition:
The supernatural Functional Gift that God gives to certain members of the body of Christ which enables them to communicate information relevant to the health and ministry of the body and its members in such a way that others will learn.

Biblical Example: Luke and Apollos

Suggested Characteristics:

1. Presents truth in a logical, systematic way.
2. Loves to validate truth by intensive research.
3. Prefers teaching believers to engaging in evangelism.
4. Feels this gift is foundational to the operation of other gifts.
5. Earnestly desires to explain biblical principles to others.
6. Is concerned to help others learn what the Bible teaches about life.
7. Gets excited about acquiring knowledge out of God's Word.
8. Tends to draw illustrations and applications from biblical sources rather than non-biblical ones (Acts 17:2-3; 18:28).

Suggested Potential Weaknesses:

1. Emphasizes accuracy at the expense of application. Lacks warmth.
2. Bores listeners with unnecessary details.
3. May appear to be more dependent on research of others than on the Holy Spirit.
4. Becomes proud of knowledge.
5. Lets teaching get ahead of living.
6. Concentrates on "pet" doctrines.

7. Gives impression that he or she is the only valid source of truth.
8. Criticizes teaching of others due to petty differences.
9. Discounts the wisdom of the uneducated.

Suggested Uses:

1. Sunday school teacher
2. Visitation
3. Youth worker
4. Bible study leader
5. Discipleship coordinator
6. Training coordinator
7. Administrator of education
8. Children's church leader

9. Gift of Exhortation/Encouragement

Biblical Example: Paul and Barnabas

Suggested Definition:

The supernatural Functional Gift that God gives to certain members of the body of Christ to encourage, stimulate faith and counsel, and support and strengthen those in the body of Christ in such a way that they feel helped and healed.

Suggested Characteristics:

1. Loves to prescribe precise steps of action to aid personal growth (Romans 12:1-2).
2. Enjoys working with those eager to follow steps of action (Proverbs 13:10).
3. Will encourage others to develop in their personal ministry (Philippians 3:17).
4. Finds truth in experience and validates it with Scripture (James 1:22).
5. Loves to do personal counseling (1 Timothy 4:11-16).

6. Dislikes teaching that is not followed by practical application (James 2:18).
7. Accepts people where they are. Non-judgmental (1 Corinthians 4:4-5).
8. Loves to encourage others to live victoriously (Philippians 4:6; Acts 11:23).
9. Usually completes what is started (2 Timothy 4:7).
10. Expects a lot from self and others (Ephesians 4:1; Galatians 6:9).

Suggested Potential Weaknesses:

1. Tends to interrupt others in eagerness to give advice or opinion.
2. Prefers to witness with the life rather than through verbal witnessing.
3. Will use Scriptures out of context in order to make a point.
4. May be "cut-and-dried" in prescribing steps of action to counsel.
5. Emphasis on steps of action may appear to oversimplify the problem.
6. Can become overly confident in prescribed steps of action.

Suggested Uses:

1. Greeter
2. Counselor
3. Discipleship
4. Altar worker
5. Parking lot attendant

Week Six

Giving, Administration, and Showing Mercy Gifts

10. Gift of Giving

Biblical Example: Matthew and Abraham

Suggested Definition:

The supernatural Functional Gift that God gives to certain members of the body of Christ to contribute their material resources to the work of the Lord with liberality and cheerfulness.

Suggested Characteristics:

1. Ability to make wise purchases and investments in order to set aside more resources for the Lord (Matthew 25:14-23).
2. Desire to give quietly to effective ministries and projects (Matthew 6:4).
3. Attempt to use his giving to motivate others to give (Luke 6:38).
4. Alertness to valid needs he fears others may overlook (Proverbs 19:7; 22:9).
5. Enjoyment in meeting needs without pressure of appeals (Matthew 10:8).
6. Joy when his gift is an answer to another's prayer (2 Corinthians 9:7).
7. Concern that his gift be of high quality (Matthew 2:11; Luke 7:37, 38).
8. Desire to feel a part of the work or person to whom he gives (Luke 8:1-3; Acts 4:37).
9. Readiness to give regularly (2 Corinthians 8:7; 1 Corinthians 16:2).

Suggested Potential Weaknesses:

1. Need to deal with large sums of money may appear to focus on temporal values.
2. Desire to give to a ministry may appear as attempt to control the work or person.
3. Attempt to encourage others to give may appear as lack of generosity and unnecessary pressure.

4. Lack of response to pressure appeals may appear to be lack of generosity.
5. Living personally frugal may appear to others as selfishness in not meeting friends' or relatives' needs.
6. Giving out of hope of big gain might cross line of trusting God to forcing Him.
7. The desire to abuse this gift to get from the saints.

Suggested Uses:

1. Treasurer
2. Board/Committee
3. Missions
4. Relief agencies

11. Gift of Administration/Government/Leadership

Biblical Example: Joseph and Nehemiah

Suggested Definition:
The supernatural Functional Gift that God gives to certain members of the body of Christ to plan, organize, and direct the activities to implement His will.

Suggested Characteristics:

1. Ability to see overall picture and clarify long-range goals (Nehemiah 1:2-3; 2:5).
2. Motivation to organize what he is responsible for.
3. Desire to complete tasks as quickly as possible.
4. Awareness of resources available to complete a task.
5. Ability to know what can and cannot be delegated (Nehemiah 4:13).
6. Tendency to stand on sidelines until those in charge tell him to take over.
7. Tendency to assume responsibility if no structured leadership exists.

8. Willingness to endure reactions from workers in order to accomplish ultimate tasks (Nehemiah 4:4-18).
9. Fulfillment in seeing others coming together and enjoying a completed task (Nehemiah 7:1-2; 8:1-18).
10. Desire to move on to a new challenge when a previous task is completed.
11. Willingness to be accountable to the whole body, seeking and executing its guidelines.

Suggested Potential Weaknesses:

1. Delegating responsibilities may appear as laziness.
2. Willingness to endure reaction may appear as callousness.
3. Neglect in explaining why tasks must be done may prompt workers to think they are being misused.
4. Viewing people as resources may make it appear that projects are more important than people.
5. The desire to complete tasks swiftly may appear to be insensitivity to the schedules, weariness, and priorities of workers.

Suggested Uses:

1. Cell groups leader
2. Sunday school superintendent
3. Organize special events
4. Organize small groups
5. Organize ministries
6. Coordinator

12. Gift of Showing Mercy

Biblical Example: John the Beloved and the Good Samaritan

Suggested Definition:

The supernatural Functional Gift that God gives to certain members of the body of Christ to respond wholeheartedly with extraordinary compassion to those who are in need, particularly spiritually.

Suggested Characteristics:

1. Easily discerns the motives of people (1 John 4:1-3).
2. Looks for the good in people. Is non-critical (Jude 23).
3. Senses the spiritual and emotional atmosphere of a group (Philemon 7).
4. Is attracted to people who are hurting or in distress (1 John 3:17, 18).
5. Wants to remove hurts and relieve distress (1 John 3:19-20).
6. Is motivated to help people to have right relationships with one another (1 John 2:9-11).
7. Loves opportunities to give place to others (Romans 12:8).
8. Takes care with words and actions to avoid hurting others (1 John 2:1).
9. Easily detects insincerity in others (1 John 2:4).
10. Is drawn to others with the gift of compassion.
11. Is thoughtful. Loves to do things for others. Remembers special occasions (1 John 3:18).
12. Trusts. Expects others to be honest and reliable (3 John 5, 6).
13. Lacks firmness unless it's seen how it will bring benefit (3 John 9-11).

Suggested Potential Weaknesses:

1. Tends to be indecisive.
2. Tends to be guided by emotions more than logic.
3. The tenderness and sensitivity can cause them to take up another person's offense.
4. Can be easily hurt by others.
5. Can let the empathy for the suffering of others infiltrate own mind or body.
6. Must be very careful in ministering to opposite sex. Compassion can be misinterpreted.
7. May exhibit pity when the person in need requires exhortation or reproof and therefore may hinder healing or growth.
8. May concentrate more on the physical needs than on helping the people spiritually.
9. May concentrate more on soul winning and ignore the physical needs.

Suggested Uses:

1. Evangelism/soul winning
2. Outreach
3. Altar worker
4. Prison and hospital visitation
5. Visitation
6. Missions

Week Seven

Word of Wisdom, Word of Knowledge, and Gift of Faith

13. Word of Wisdom

Suggested Definition:

The supernatural Manifestation Gift that God gives to members of the body of Christ that enables them to receive instant insight on how a situation, a scripture, a teaching, a revelation (word of knowledge, prophecy) may best be applied to a specific situation or need arising in the body of Christ, or how a given situation or need is to be resolved or helped or healed.

Suggested Characteristics:

1. Is a practical problem solver (Genesis 41:35-37; 1 Kings 3:16-28; Acts 16:1-4).
2. Receives understanding from the Lord about the best way to handle a situation or problem (Acts 15:28).
3. Often senses an awareness of how to pray or otherwise act to particular needs (Acts 16:25-31).

Suggested Potential Weaknesses:

1. May tend to appear to be authoritative in telling others how to act.
2. Tends to make decisions too quickly.
3. Can become proud of having this gift.
4. Can use gift to manipulate people or unwittingly cause others to be dependent upon the one with the gift.
5. Could cause problems if gift is not shared in love.

Suggested Uses:

1. Board/Committee
2. Visitation
3. Discipleship
4. Teaching

14. Word of Knowledge

Suggested Definition:

The supernatural Manifestation Gift that God gives to certain members of the body of Christ which consists of a revelation of facts about a person or situation, which is not learned through the efforts of the natural mind, but is a fragment of knowledge freely given by God, disclosing the truth which the Spirit wishes to be made known concerning a particular person or situation.

Suggested Characteristics:

1. Is able to speak forth by divine revelation the specific facts about a situation (Matthew 21:2; Mark 14:13-15; Acts 5:1-3).
2. Is able to reveal to individuals or groups their specific needs (John 4:16-26; Acts 9:11-12, 17; Luke 5:2-4).
3. Receives supernatural facts or information (Matthew 16:16-17; Acts 10:19).
4. Is able to discern the voice of the Lord (Acts 10:17-23).
5. Shows humility and childlikeness (Luke 10:21).
6. Is able to discern what is in a man's heart (Acts 14:9; John 2:24).

Suggested Potential Weaknesses:

1. May have false impulses that are contradictory to God's Word or revelation.
2. Must take extreme care in the case of secrets revealed.
3. Might have a tendency to use acquired knowledge through observation or conversation and reveal it as a Word of Knowledge.

4. Might try to operate on one's own experience of God and His ways rather than supernatural revelation.
5. Can become proud.

Suggested Uses:

1. Bible teaching
2. Premarital counseling
3. Counseling
4. Teaching

15. Gift of Faith

Suggested Definition:

The supernatural Manifestation Gift that God gives to certain members of the body of Christ which enables them to discern with extraordinary confidence the will and purposes of God for the future of His work.

Suggested Characteristics:

1. Is more interested in the future than history (Acts 27:25).
2. Is unmoved by circumstances, suffering, or obstacles (Acts 13:46-52).
3. Has great trust in God (Acts 14:8-10).
4. Shows a positive attitude, may be a visionary, dreamer, promoter (Acts 9:27).
5. Is very courageous (Acts 6:5; 7:1-60; 27:25).
6. Senses the moment when "prayer of faith" is needed (Acts 3:1-10).
7. Is goal-centered (Acts 27:25).

Suggested Potential Weaknesses:

1. May be viewed as non-realist because of positive attitudes.
2. May become impatient when others don't have the same kind of positive faith outlook.
3. May have a difficult time understanding "the system" and why it works as it does to slow down progress.
4. May exercise Gift of Faith without works.
5. Is often irritated by criticism because he/she has assurance of knowing God's will.

Suggested Uses:

1. Board member
2. Prayer ministries
3. Building projects
4. Altar worker
5. Finance committee

Week Eight
Healing and Miracles Gifts

16. Gifts of Healing

Suggested Definition:

The supernatural Manifestation Gift that God gives to certain members of the body of Christ which enables them to serve as human intermediaries, through whom it pleases God to cure various illnesses and restore health supernaturally, and is often used in conjunction with the Word of Knowledge and the Gift of Faith.

Suggested Characteristics:

1. Enjoys and senses the need to pray for the healing of the sick (1 Corinthians 14:1; John 5:14-16).
2. Has a great faith that God can heal apart from natural means (Acts 3:6).
3. Has compassion on others who are sick or suffering and is willing to take time in ministering healing to them (Acts 3:6; 9:32-42).
4. Often the gifts of healing come to the person being healed (Paul being healed and then healer).
5. Understands that Jesus is the healer and hence faith is directed away from himself (Acts 3:12).

Suggested Potential Weaknesses:

1. Temptation to pride — boasting after a clear manifestation of the power of God.
2. Tendency to become critical toward others who try to rationalize sickness or who do not believe in God's power to heal.
3. Discouragement if healing does not take place.
4. Temptation to stop listening to God and operate in his own strength or in the flesh.
5. Temptation to doubt God's power, especially with a drastic sickness or illness.
6. Temptation to rush through prayer for the sick and tell the person to "just receive your healing."

Suggested Uses:

1. Healing ministries
2. Visitation
3. Prayer ministries
4. Altar work

17. Gift of Miracles

Suggested Definition:

The supernatural Manifestation Gift that God gives to certain members of the body of Christ that enables them to serve as intermediaries, through whom it pleases God to intervene in the regular operations of nature.

Suggested Characteristics:

1. Often sees supernatural miracles (Acts 5:1-10; 13:8-11).
2. Has a great interest in supernaturalism rather than naturalism (Acts 20:9-12).
3. Is compassionate.
4. Can point to specific instances where his prayers resulted in miracles (Acts 9:32-41).

Suggested Potential Weaknesses:

1. Can be easily abused through selfishness or pride.
2. May feel that everything is OK between him and the Lord because he has done miracles (Matthew. 7:21).

Suggested Uses:

1. Prayer ministries
2. Hospital visitation
3. Missions
4. Altar work

Week Nine

Gifts of Prophecy (Manifestation) and Discernment of Spirits

18. Gift of Prophecy

Suggested Definition:

The supernatural Manifestation Gift that God gives to certain members of the body of Christ, which enables them to receive and communicate a message from God to man through a divinely anointed utterance.

Suggested Characteristics:

1. Builds up the community. The whole purpose is positive, although there may be admonition and warning, even exhortation, to desist from some evil. Has a real lifting power and gives real light on the truth to those who hear.
2. Finds consent and agreement in the minds and hearts of others in the community. There should be a prevailing sense in the community that the prophecy was divinely inspired.
3. May be spoken in a variety of ways as the Lord Himself wills it.
4. It comes forth in power of the Spirit of God.
5. Spontaneity marks such an occasion, and the words are divinely inspired.
6. The prophetic word should be given in an orderly manner (1 Corinthians 14:26-40).
7. Not infallible and the utterance must be judged by the infallible Word of God. The person should be humble enough to allow his word to be judged (1 Corinthians 14:29). If it is the mind of God, there is nothing to fear.
8. Prophecy has a vital connection with faith; the individual must prophesy according to the measure of faith (Romans 12:6).
9. Paul has a tendency to prefer prophecy to other gifts (1 Corinthians 14:1).
10. It stays on the sober ground of faith (cf. Romans 12:6). God gives and the believer makes responsible use of the gifts. Prophecy declares God's counsel openly (1 Corinthians 14:5) and edifies the whole Church, although there may be

exhortation and admonition and warning to desist from some evil (14:2-3).

11. It may convict nonbelievers (1 Corinthians 14:24-25).
12. Prophecy should be harmonious with God's Word; it must not take away from nor add to Scripture, but should intensify and quicken that which already has been given to us from God (1 Corinthians 14:27-33; Revelations 22:19).
13. It may be spoken in a variety of ways; it is the Lord speaking through a human vessel (1 Corinthians 14:3-6, 27-33), in the power of the Holy Spirit (12:4-11).
14. Speaks as one speaking the very words of God (1 Peter 4:10-11).

Suggested Potential Weaknesses:

1. Deals with things that do not edify and are designed to puff up hearers and to lead them into error.
2. If you are not humble enough to allow your prophecy to be judged, it is as surely wrong as you are wrong.
3. If you hear any voices that make you think that you are superior to those whom God has put in the church to rule the church, watch out, for this is surely of the devil.
4. Forgets to praise partial progress (due to goal consciousness).
5. Can be misused if not properly judged (1 Corinthians 14:29).
6. Not all prophecies may be of God (2 Corinthians 11:3-4, 13-15; 2 Thessalonians 2:1-2).
7. The person giving the prophecy may be forbidden or hindered by leaders or the congregation (1 Thessalonians 5:19-20).

Suggested Uses:

1. Sharing a word from God
2. Intercession
3. Spiritual gifts advisor
4. Prison and jail ministries
5. Inner city ministry
6. Ministry at the altar
7. Ministry in cell groups
8. Boards and committees

19. Gift of Discernment of Spirits

Suggested Definition:

The supernatural Manifestation Gift that God gives to certain members of the body of Christ that enables them to have supernatural insight into the realm of spirits (whether they are of God, Satan, or human).

Suggested Characteristics:

1. Can tell good spirits from evil spirits and right spirits from wrong spirits (1 John 4:1).
2. Can understand the spirits operating (1 Corinthians 14:29; Mark 5:6-13).
3. Can discern the spiritual condition of individuals (Acts 16:16-18).

Suggested Potential Weaknesses:

1. Can be viewed as a suspicion rather than a perception.
2. Tends to be judgmental.
3. To falsely deliver people from spirits could cause more problems than it cures.
4. An *incorrect* judgment of a person by someone assuming he/she has the gift of discernment, (or an understandable mistake by one who legitimately possesses this gift), could cause great harm to that individual and to the body of Christ.
5. Has a tendency to forget using the authority of Jesus' name (Jude 8-10; 2 Peter 2:1-11) and opening the door to spirit activity in his/her own life.
6. May have a "quick fix" mentality regarding evil (Luke 11:24-26).

Suggested Uses:

1. Board member
2. Evangelism
3. Visitation
4. Worship

Week 10

Tongues and Interpretation Gifts

20. Gift of Tongues

Suggested Definition:

The supernatural Manifestation Gift that God gives to certain members of the body of Christ which enables them to (a) speak in a language unlearned by the speaker naturally, and/or (b) to receive and communicate an immediate message of God to His people through a divinely-anointed utterance for the interpretation in a language unlearned by the speaker.

Suggested Characteristics:

1. Has publicly spoken in an unlearned language or in ecstatic utterances (Acts 2:4).
2. Speaking in tongues is sometimes directed toward God and is a declaration of praise (1 Corinthians 14:2, 16, 17; Acts 2:11; 10:46).
3. Tongues consist of speaking mysteries in the Spirit (1 Corinthians 14:2).
4. Tongues edify the person doing the speaking (1 Corinthians 14:4,17).
5. The individual must do the speaking, although the Holy Spirit gives the words (Acts 2:4).
6. This gift may be expressed as a form of prayer and also as a way of singing (1 Corinthians 14:14,15; Romans 8:26-27)).
7. The gift consists of different kinds of tongues, which suggests that there may be a variety of tongues uttered (1 Corinthians 12:10).
8. This gift is a sign to unbelievers (1 Corinthians 14:22).

9. The use of this gift has a strong relationship to the gift of the interpretation of tongues. For example in the context of a church service:
   a. The one who speaks in a tongue should pray that he may interpret what he says (1 Corinthians 14:13) or know that someone present will be able to interpret or otherwise just speak quietly to God (1 Corinthians 14:28).
   b. It is the accompanying gift of the "interpretation of tongues" that allows the church to be edified (1 Corinthians14:5-19).
   c. Also, tongues and interpretation should be limited to three people and should be done orderly (1 Corinthians 14:27).
10. Tongues *can* also be a sign of the initial reception of the Holy Spirit (Acts 2:4; 10:44-46; 19:6).
11. Tongues as an initial sign of the reception of the Holy Spirit require no interpretation (Acts 2).
12. Interpretation is not required in private use (1 Corinthians 14:14).
13. Tongues as an initial sign (on the Day of Pentecost) are called prophecy (Acts 2:14-18).
14. Singing in the Spirit is meant as singing in tongues (1 Corinthians 14:13-16).
15. Speaking in tongues is sometimes speaking in a known language yet unknown to the speaker (Acts 2:4-6).
16. Has boldness to speak forth.

Suggested Potential Weaknesses:

1. Uncontrolled use and overemphasis can create confusion within local church.
2. Tends to force this gift on others.
3. May be viewed as too much "experience-oriented."

Suggested Uses:

1. Worship
2. Board member
3. Prayer ministries
4. Missions

21. Gift of Interpretation

Suggested Definition:

The supernatural Manifestation Gift that God gives to certain members of the body of Christ, which enables them to make known in the vernacular the message of one who speaks in tongues.

Suggested Characteristics:

1. Has interpreted tongues with the result that the body of Christ was edified, exhorted, or comforted (1 Corinthians 14:3, 26).
2. Has sensitivity to the Spirit's promptings; is yielded (1 Corinthians 14:15).
3. Has sensed an understanding of what God is saying while a message in tongues is given (1 Corinthians 14:5).

Suggested Potential Weaknesses:

1. Seems to be too subjective rather than objective.
2. It is possible that the words of a presumed interpretation are not given by the Holy Spirit (but from human spirit or diabolical spirit).
3. Also it may be that the apparent interpretation is a prophecy.

Suggested Uses:

1. Worship
2. Missions
3. Prayer ministries
4. Board member

Notes

1. Michael Green, *I Believe in the Holy Spirit* (London: Hodder and Stoughton, 1975), p. 198.
2. J. Rodman Williams, "Class Notes," *Holy Spirit: Presence and Power*, Regent University, Spring Quarter, 1991.
3. Leslie B. Flynn, *19 Gifts of the Spirit: Which Do You Have? Are You Using Them?* (Wheaton: Victor Books, 1974), p. 32.
4. Marilyn Hickey, *Seven Gifts to Success* (Denver: Life For Laymen, n.d.).
5. David Pytches, *Spiritual Gifts in the Local Church* (Minneapolis: Bethany House Publishers, 1985), pp. 57-61.
6. W.T. Purkiser, *The Gifts of the Spirit* (Kansas City: Beacon Hill Press of Kansas City, 1975), pp. 17-18, 25-48.
7. Ralph M. Riggs, *The Spirit Himself* (Springfield: Gospel Publishing House, 1949), pp. 113-120.
8. Harold Horton, *The Gifts of the Spirit* (Springfield: Gospel Publishing House, 1934), pp. 25-26.
9. Raymond W. Hurn, et. al., *Finding Your Ministry: A Study of the Fruit and Gifts of the Spirit* (Kansas City: Beacon Hill Press of Kansas City, 1979), pp. 21, 88-94.
10. Peter Wagner lists as spiritual gifts the following which are difficult to substantiate biblically: celibacy, philanthropy, hospitality, exorcism, prayer/intercession, poverty, martyrdom, healing, music, art, drama, *ad infinitum.*
11. Mark 16:17 says *exorcism* is a part of the signs that follow Christians, and would more likely be a part of the gift of miracles or the gifts of healing.
12. Kevin J. Conner, *The Church in the New Testament* (Portland, Oregon: Conner Publications, 1982), p. 145.
13. Daniel B. Wallaby, "The Semantic Range of the Article-Noun-Kai-Noun Plural Construction in the New Testament," *Grace Theological Journal*, 4:1 (1983): 59-84.
14. J. Rodman Williams, *Renewal Theology 2: Salvation, the Holy Spirit, and Christian Living* (Grand Rapids, Michigan: Zondervan Publishing House, 1990), p. 334 (footnote 55).
15. J. Rodman Williams, *Renewal Theology Volume III: The Church and Last Things*, manuscript, p. 4-137.
16. Williams, *Renewal Theology Volume III*, p. 4-138.
17. Marilyn Hickey, n.p.
18. Williams, *Renewal Theology II*, p. 346.
19. Bruce L. Bugbee, *Networking (Leader's Guide)* (Pasadena, CA: Charles E. Fuller Institute of Evangelism and Church Growth, 1989), p. 51.
20. Kevin J. Conner, *The Church in the New Testament* (Portland: Bible Temple Publishing, 1989), p. 214.
21. Frank Damazio, *The Making of a Leader* (Portland, Oregon: Trilogy Productions, 1988), p. 47.
22. While apostles may be missionaries or cross-culturally oriented, this is not always the case; as in Peter or better yet James. Yet, the very nature of the work of many missionaries down through the history of the Christian Church has demanded of them a significant enabling in the ministry of an apostle.
23. Leslie B. Flynn, pp. 42-43.
24. Donald Gee, *The Ministry-Gifts of Christ* (Springfield, MO: Gospel Publishing House, 1930), p. 29.
25. Howard A. Snyder, *The Community of the King* (Downers Grove, IL: Inter-Varsity Press, 1977), pp. 87-88.
26. B. E. Underwood, *Spiritual Gifts: Ministries and Manifestations* (Franklin Springs: GA: Advocate Press [now LifeSprings Resources], 1984), pp. 21-22.
27. C. Peter Wagner, *Your Spiritual Gifts Can Help Your Church Grow* (Ventura, CA: Regal Books, 1979), p. 208.
28. Conner, p. 214.
29. Damazio, p. 47.
30. Hobart Freeman, *An Introduction to the Old Testament* (Chicago: Moody Press, 1968), pp. 49ff.

31. Underwood, p. 22.
32. Bugbee, p. 51.
33. Conner, p. 214.
34. Damazio, p. 47.
35. Flynn, p. 57.
36. Underwood, p. 54.
37. Wagner, p. 173.
38. W. E. Vine, *Vine's Expository Dictionary* (Old Tappan: Fleming H. Revell Company, 1966), p. 167.
39. Bugbee, p. 53.
40. Conner, p. 214.
41. Damazio, p. 47.
42. Flynn, pp. 66-70.
43. Wagner, p. 143.
44. Bugbee, p. 33.
45. Conner, p. 214.
46. Damazio, p. 47.
47. Wagner, p. 127.
48. Bugbee, p. 33.
49. Conner, p. 214.
50. Damazio, p. 47.
51. Flynn, p. 53.
52. Don and Katie Fortune, *Discover Your God-Given Gifts* (Tarrytown, NY: Fleming H. Revell Co., 1987), pp. 46.
53. B. E. Underwood, *The Gifts of the Spirit* (Franklin Springs, GA: Advocate Press [now LifeSprings Resources], 1967), p. 41.
54. Wagner, p. 228.
55. Don and Katie Fortune, pp. 61, 67.
56. Bill Gothard, *Additional Insights On Understanding Spiritual Gifts* (Washington, D.C.: Institute in Basic Youth Conflicts, 1981), n.p.
57. Hickey, op. cit., n.p.
58. Bugbee, p. 52.
59. Conner, p. 215.
60. Damazio, p. 50.
61. Flynn, p. 100.
62. Wagner, pp. 224-226.
63. Fortune and Fortune, pp. 88, 93.
64. Gothard, op. cit.
65. Hickey, n.p.
66. Bugbee, p. 54.
67. Conner, p. 214.
68. Damazio, p. 48.
69. Flynn, pp. 74, 77.
70. David Allen Hubbard, *Unwrapping Your Spiritual Gifts* (Waco: Word Books, 1985), p. 47.
71. Wagner, p. 127.
72. Fortune and Fortune, pp. 108, 112.
73. Gothard, op. cit.
74. Hickey, n.p.
75. Bugbee, p. 35.
76. Conner, p. 215.
77. Damazio, p. 48.
78. Flynn, pp. 82-83.
79. Wagner, p. 154.

80. Fortune and Fortune, pp. 128, 133.
81. Gothard, op. cit.
82. Hickey, n.p.
83. Bugbee, p. 39.
84. Conner, p. 215.
85. Damazio, p. 48.
86. Flynn, p. 117.
87. Wagner, p. 31.
88. Fortune and Fortune, pp. 150, 155.
89. Gothard, op. cit.
90. Hickey, n.p.
91. Bugbee, p. 53.
92. Conner, p. 215.
93. Damazio, pp. 48, 50.
94. Flynn, p. 127.
95. Underwood, *Ministries and Manifestations*, p. 48.
96. Wagner, pp. 156, 262.
97. Fortune and Fortune, pp. 171, 176.
98. Gothard, op. cit.
99. Hickey, n.p.
100. Bugbee, p. 37.
101. Conner, p. 215.
102. Damazio, p. 48.
103. Flynn, p. 133.
104. Wagner, p. 223.
105. Fortune and Fortune, pp. 193, 198.
106. Gothard, op. cit.
107. Hickey, n.p.
108. Bugbee, p. 42.
109. Conner, p. 214.
110. Damazio, p. 49.
111. Flynn, p. 92.
112. Riggs, pp. 127-133.
113. Wagner, p. 220.
114. Williams, *Renewal Theology 2*, p. 350.
115. Bugbee, p. 53.
116. Conner, p. 214.
117. Damazio, p. 49.
118. Flynn, pp. 90-91.
119. Riggs, p. 126.
120. Wagner, p. 218.
121. Williams, *Renewal Theology 2*, pp. 356-357.
122. Bugbee, p. 37.
123. Conner, p. 214.
124. Damazio, p. 49.
125. Flynn, p. 133.
126. Riggs, p. 144.
127. Wagner, p. 158.
128. Williams, *Renewal Theology 2*, pp. 358-364.
129. Bugbee, p. 52.
130. Conner, p. 214.
131. Damazio, p. 49.

132. Flynn, p. 170.
133. Riggs, p. 139.
134. Wagner, p. 238.
135. Williams, *Renewal Theology 2*, pp. 367-368.
136. Bugbee, p. 53.
137. Conner, p. 214.
138. Damazio, p. 49.
139. Flynn, p. 161.
140. Riggs, p. 148.
141. Wagner, pp. 237-238.
142. Williams, *Renewal Theology 2*, p. 375.
143. Bugbee, p. 33.
144. Conner, p. 214.
145. Damazio, p. 47.
146. Flynn, p. 53.
147. Horton, p. 159.
148. R.M. Riggs, p. 154.
149. B.E. Underwood, *The Gifts of the Spirit*, p. 41.
150. Wagner, p. 228.
151. Williams, p. 382.
152. Bugbee, p. 51.
153. Conner, p. 214.
154. Flynn, p. 153.
155. Damazio, p. 50.
156. Riggs, p. 136.
157. Wagner, p. 102.
158. Williams, *Renewal Theology 2*, p. 389.
159. Bugbee, p. 54.
160. Conner, p. 215.
161. Damazio, p. 50.
162. Flynn, p. 180.
163. Riggs, p. 163-166.
164. Wagner, p. 233.
165. Bugbee, p. 53.
166. Conner, p. 215.
167. Damazio, p. 50.
168. Flynn, p. 180.
169. Riggs, p. 167.
170. Wagner, p. 235.
171. Williams, *Renewal Theology 2*, p. 403.
172. Bugbee, pp. 47, 73.
173. Flynn, p. 22.
174. Ray Stedman, *Body Life* (Glendale, CA: Regal Publishing Co., 1977), p. 54.
175. Bugbee, p. 73.
176. C. Peter Wagner, pp. 113-133.
177. Wagner, op. cit., p. 123.
178. Kenneth Cain Kinghorn, *Discovering Your Spiritual Gifts: A Personal Method* (Wilmore, KY: Frances Asbury Publishing Company, Inc., 1981), pp. 8, 9.
179. Kenneth O. Gangel, *Feeding and Leading* (USA: Victor Books, 1989), pp. 133-145, 241-246.

Bibliography

Aden, Leroy and J. Harold Ellens, eds. *The Church and Pastoral Care*. Grand Rapids, Michigan: Baker Book House, 1988.

Baxter, R. E. *Gifts of the Spirit*. Kregel Publication, 1983.

Bennett, Dennis and Rita. *The Holy Spirit and You*. Plainfield: Logos International, 1971.

Bittlinger, Arnold. *Gifts and Graces: A Commentary on I Corinthians 12-14*. English Translation. Grand Rapids, 1967.

Borchert, Gerald L. and Andrew D. Lester, eds. *Spiritual Dimensions of Pastoral Care: Witness to the Ministry of Wayne E. Oates*. Philadelphia: Westminster Press, 1985.

Bryant, C. V. *Rediscovering the Charismata: Building up the Body of Christ*. Word Books, 1986.

Bugbee, Bruce L. *Networking (Leader's Guide)*. Pasadena, CA: Charles E. Fuller Institute of Evangelism and Church Growth, 1989.

Chisolm, Gloria. *Encourage One Another*. Word Books, 1986.

Conn, Charles W. *A Balanced Church*. Cleveland, TN: Pathway Press, 1975.

Conner, Kevin J. *The Church in the New Testament*. Portland: Bible Temple Publishing, 1989.

Criswell, W. A. *The Holy Spirit in Today's World*. Grand Rapids: Zondervan, 1976.

Damazio, Frank. *The Making of a Leader*. Portland, Oregon: Trilogy Productions, 1988.

Fee, Gordon D. *The First Epistle to the Corinthians*. Grand Rapids: Eerdmans, 1987.

Flynn, L. B. *Nineteen Gifts of the Spirit: Which Do You Have? Are You Using Them?*. Wheaton, IL: Victor Books, 1974.

Fortune, Don and Katie. *Discover Your God-Given Gifts*. Old Tappan, NJ: Fleming Revel Co., 1987.

Freeman, Hobart. *An Introduction to the Old Testament*. Chicago: Moody Press, 1968.

Gangel, Kenneth O. *Feeding and Leading*. USA: Victor Books, 1989.

Gee, D. *Concerning Spiritual Gifts, a Series of Bible Studies*. Springfield: Gospel Publishing House, 1972.

Gee, D. *The Ministry-Gifts of Christ*. Springfield, MO: Gospel Publishing House, 1930.

Gee, D. *Now That You've Been Baptized in the Spirit*. 1972.

Gee, D. *Spiritual Gifts in the Work of the Ministry Today.* Springfield: Gospel Publishing House.

Gelpi, Donald. *Charism and Sacrament. . .A Theology of Christian Conversion.* New York: Paulist Press, 1976.

Goetchius, E.V.N. and C. P. Price. *The Gifts of God.* Welton, CT: Moorehouse Barlow, 1984.

Gothard, Bill. *Additional Insights on Understanding Spiritual Conflicts.* Washington, D.C.: Institute in Basic Youth Conflicts, 1981.

Green, Michael. *I Believe in the Holy Spirit.* London: Hodder and Stoughton, 1975.

Hagin, K. E. *The Gift of Prophecy.* Faith Library Publishing, 1969.

Hagin, K. E. *The Ministry of a Prophet.* K. Hagin Ministries, 1968.

Hickey, Marilyn. *Seven Gifts to Success.* Denver: Life for Laymen, n.d.

Hodge, Charles. *A Commentary on 1 & 2 Corinthians.* London: Billing and Sons, 1974.

Hodges, Melvin. *Spiritual Gifts.* Springfield, MO: Gospel Publishing House, 1964.

Horton, H. *Gifts of the Spirit.* Springfield: Gospel Publishing House, 1975.

Hubbard, D. A. *Unwrapping Your Spiritual Gifts.* Word Books, 1985.

Hurding, Roger F. *Christian Care and Counseling: A Practical Guide.* Morehouse-Barlow Co., 1983.

Hurn, Raymond W. et. al. *Finding Your Ministry: A Study of the Fruit and Gifts of the Spirit.* Kansas City: Beacon Hill Press of Kansas City, 1979.

Kemp, Charles F. *The Caring Pastor: An Introduction to Pastoral Counseling.* Abingdon, 1985.

King, George Davis. *Lessons on the Holy Spirit.* Nashville: Broadman Press, 1988.

Kinghorn, Kenneth Cain. *Discovering Your Spiritual Gifts: A Personal Method.* Wilmore: Frances Asbury Publishing Company, Inc., 1981.

Mitchell, Marcia. *Giftedness: Discovering Your Areas of Strength.* Bethany House Publishers, 1988.

Owen, D. R. *Release Your Gifts and Help Your Church Grow.* Fuller Evangelistic, 1984.

Palma, Anthony D. *The Spirit: God in Action.* Springfield: Gospel Publishing House, 1974.

Purkiser, W. T. *The Gifts of the Spirit.* Kansas City: Beacon Hill Press of Kansas City, 1975.

Pytches, David. *Spiritual Gifts in the Local Church.* Minneapolis: Bethany House Publishers, 1985.

Riggs, R. M. *The Spirit Himself.* Springfield, MO: Gospel Publishing House, 1949.

Sanders, J. Oswald. *The Holy Spirit and His Gifts.* Grand Rapids: Zondervan Publishing House, 1970.

Schatzmann, Siegfried S. *A Pauline Theology of Charismata.* Peabody, MA: Hendrickson, 1987.

Slater, Michael. *Stretcher Bearers.* Regal Books, 1985.

Snyder, Howard A. *The Community of the King.* Downers Grove, IL: Inter-Varsity Press, 1977.

Stedman, Ray. *Body Life.* Glendale, CA: Regal Publishing Co., 1977.

Stifler, J. M. *The Epistle to the Romans.* New York: Revell, 1897.

Stowe, Eugene L. *Ministry of Shepherding: A Study of Pastoral Practice.* Beacon Hill Press, 1976.

Underwood, B. E. *The Gift of the Spirit.* Franklin Springs, GA: Advocate Press (now LifeSprings Resources), 1967.

Underwood, B. E. *Spiritual Gifts: Ministries and Manifestation.* Franklin Springs, GA: Advocate Press (now LifeSprings Resources), 1984.

Vine, W. E. *Vine's Expository Dictionary.* Old Tappan: Fleming H. Revell Company, 1966.

Wagner, C. Peter. *Your Spiritual Gifts Can Help Your Church Grow.* Ventura, CA: Regal Books, 1979.

Wallaby, Daniel B. "The Semantic Range of the Article-Noun-Kai-Noun Plural Construction in the New Testament." *Grace Theological Journal*, 4:1 (1983).

Wigglesworth, S. *Ever Increasing Faith.* Springfield: Gospel Publishing House, 1971.

Williams, J. Rodman. *Renewal Theology 2: Salvation, the Holy Spirit, and Christian Living.* Grand Rapids, Michigan: Zondervan Publishing House, 1990.

Williams, J. Rodman. *Renewal Theology Volume III: The Church and Last Things*, manuscript.

Wuest, K. S. *Romans in the Greek New Testament.* Grand Rapids: Eerdmans, 1955.